Domestic Realism and the Performance of
Gender in Early Canadian Fiction

Femininity in colonial societies is a particularly contested element of the sex/gender system; while it draws on a conservative belief in universal and continuous values, it is undermined by the liberal rhetoric of freedom characteristic of the New World. *Practising Femininity* analyses the ways in which Canadian texts by Catharine Parr Traill, Susanna Moodie, Nellie McClung, Sinclair Ross, and others work to produce and naturalize femininity in a colonial setting.

Drawing on Judith Butler's definition of gender as performance, Misao Dean shows how practices which seem to transgress the feminine ideal – emigration, physical labour, autobiographical writing, work for wages, sexual desire, and suffrage activism – were justified by Canadian writers as legitimate expressions of an unvarying feminine inner self. Early Canadian writers cited a feminine gender ideal which emphasized love of home and adherence to duty; New Women and Suffrage writers attributed sexuality to a biological desire to reproduce; in the work of Sinclair Ross, the feminine ideal was moulded by prevailing Freudian models of femininity.

This study is grounded in the most important current gender theories, and will interest Canadian literary scholars, feminist historians and theoreticians, and students of women's studies.

MISAO DEAN is an associate professor in the Department of English at the University of Victoria and author of *A Different Point of View: Sara Jeannette Duncan.*

THEORY/CULTURE

General editors:
Linda Hutcheon, Gary Leonard, Jill Matus,
Janet Paterson, and Paul Perron

Practising Femininity

Domestic Realism and the Performance of Gender in Early Canadian Fiction

MISAO DEAN

UNIVERSITY OF TORONTO PRESS
Toronto Buffalo London

© University of Toronto Press Incorporated 1998
Toronto Buffalo London
Printed in Canada

ISBN 0-8020-4312-7 (cloth)
ISBN 0-8020-8138-X (paper)

Printed on acid-free paper

Canadian Cataloguing in Publication Data

Dean, Misao
Practising femininity : domestic realism and the performance of
gender in early Canadian fiction

(Theory/culture)
Includes bibliographical references and index.
ISBN 0-8020-4312-7 (bound)   ISBN 0-8020-8138-X (pbk.)

1. Canadian fiction (English) – History and criticism.*   2. Women in literature.
3. Femininity (Philosophy) in literature.   I. Title.   II. Series.

PS8191.W65D42 1998   C813.009352042   C97-932686-9
PR9192.6.W6D42 1998

This book has been published with the help of a grant from the Humanities and
Social Sciences Federation of Canada, using funds provided by the Social Sciences
and Humanities Research Council of Canada.

University of Toronto Press acknowledges the financial assistance to its publishing
program of the Canada Council for the Arts and the Ontario Arts Council.

for Rebecca, because she asked

Contents

Acknowledgments

Most of this book was written during a study leave from the University of Victoria, and I am grateful for both the leave and the University of Victoria Internal Research grant which supported it.

My colleagues across the country kindly responded to requests for research help and for conversation on related topics: Lorraine McMullen and Gerald Lynch at the University of Ottawa; Carole Gerson and David Stouck at Simon Fraser University; John Thurston; Michael Peterman at Trent University; Janet Friskney at Carleton University; Linda Hoad at the National Library. Thanks also to John Urquhart and *Canadian Forum*. Sneja Gunew at University of British Columbia generously read and commented on part of the manuscript.

My friends in Victoria listened to endless rants as I was working out these ideas. Lisa Surridge and Debbie and Ken Agar-Newman were patient under the onslaught of barely digested ideas. Jamie Dopp offered a detailed reading of the manuscript, and I would like to thank him most sincerely for his good humour and encouragement. Mandy Ostick checked the sources and proofread, and Celeste Derksen prepared the index. I am particularly grateful to my first best reader, Gerry Walsh, for his belief in me and my 'bad-tempered book.'

Somewhat different versions of chapters 2 and 5 were published as 'Concealing Her Blue Stockings: Femininity and Self-Representation in Susanna Moodie's Autobiographical Works,' in *Re-Siting Queen's English*, ed. Helen Tiffin and Gillian Whitlock (Amsterdam: Editions Rodopi, 1992); and 'Voicing the Voiceless: Language and Genre in Nellie McClung's Fiction and Her Autobiography,' *Atlantis* 15.1 (Fall 1989): 65–75.

Practising Femininity

Introduction: Practising Femininity

In Mary Pratt's painting *Child with Two Adults*, a newborn baby is being bathed in a large, decorated china bowl. The bowl sits upon a linen cloth with embroidered and scalloped edging; the angle of view places the child in the centre of the action, situated below the viewer and within easy reach. The child's head is supported by the left hand of an adult who leans in from the upper left corner, right hand gently splashing warm water on the child's leg; the second adult is indicated merely by a feminine hand which enters the painting at the lower right-hand edge, situated in such a way that it seems to be coming from the viewer. This hand, in conjunction with the angle of view and the exact rendering of detail, constructs the viewer as standing above and in front of the child: a participant in this domestic christening of a female child.

Pratt's paintings provide a useful analogy to the nineteenth- and early twentieth-century Canadian prose works which are the subject of this study. Like the writing, they are realist; they conform so perfectly to currently accepted conventions for the representation of the material world that some viewers mistake them for photographs, and some commentators judge them to be simply commercial. Like the writing, they are largely domestic in subject matter; Pratt's still lifes of glass and china bowls, fish, poultry and meat, table settings, and wedding dresses celebrate the beauty, harmony, and utility to be found in domestic objects, and invest them with the human value of relationship. And like the writing, Pratt's paintings construct the viewer as subject, determined by and participating in an ideology of domestic subjectivity.

For in pointing out the extraordinary effects of light and colour in what seem to be ordinary domestic objects, these paintings signify *as* ordinary a particular kind of domestic life: heterosexual, with happy well-fed children, clean crocheted tablecloths, ceremonial marriages, food cooked in traditional ways and served on beautiful china – a domestic life which exists, for most of us, more as nostalgia than reality. Yet both the paintings and the commentary Pratt provides suggest that these images surround us/her, and that the paintings themselves represent moments stolen from the flux of an ordinary woman's day.[1] In this way, the paintings are ideological, using representations of domestic objects and practices to signify a set of beliefs about what is ordinary, and to construct the viewer/reader as a participant in those beliefs and practices.

Mary Pratt's paintings declare a realm of feminine expertise which many women still claim – the arrangement of the home, the preparation of food, the nurture of children – and show this realm to be rich in aesthetic experiences. Paintings such as *Red Currant Jelly*, *Bedroom*, and *Three Gifts* direct the viewer's eye to rich experiences of light and colour in domestic scenes, as well as to the symbolic representation of emotional states in domestic objects such as tin foil, unmade beds, and crystal bowls. The paintings inhabit the traditional sphere of feminine expertise in order to assert its substance and importance. The very 'realness' of these images, the intense richness of detail which makes viewers exclaim with wonder, is created by artifice: Pratt admits to often working from several photographs, in order to ensure that every part of the image is illuminated equally. Yet this 'realness' of material detail serves to materialize the life which the paintings designate as that of an 'ordinary' woman; the technique of realism serves the ideological function of making the picture seem natural, a window on an ordinary and self-evident femininity.

In the same way, the nineteenth- and early twentieth-century Canadian prose works which are the focus of this study signify as real a particular set of beliefs and practices about gender: more specifically, about the attributes of femininity. Each of them specifically takes Woman as its subject, and each naturalizes a particular ideology of femininity by interpellating the reader as a participant in the construction of Woman as category. They present Woman as a natural category of experience, consisting of an unvarying 'inner self' which is determined by gender; various feminine practices and behaviours are created as expressions, in different historical and economic circumstances, of that unvarying, feminine, 'inner self.' Thus, in these works Woman is a myth in Barthes's sense of the term – freed from the historical contingencies which created her, universalized and de-historicized, she is a sign whose signification seems transparent, obvious.

The ways in which such historical representations of Woman perpetuate gender oppression would seem to have been thoroughly exposed; yet the dominant readings of works by Catharine Parr Traill, Susanna Moodie, Rosanna Leprohon, Jessie Sime, Joanna Wood, Lily Dougall, Nellie McClung, and Sinclair Ross bypass this insight in order to place these writers and the representations of women they create within a progressive narrative of liberation from oppressive gender norms. The assumption underlying these readings is that while women were oppressed in the past, they have been and are struggling as active agents to free themselves, and that representations of women thus become progressively more free and accurate as literature progresses from the nineteenth to the twentieth century. Such readings rest upon the theoretical assumption that representations of women in early Canadian literature are distortions of women's real lives, created by literary convention or by stereotypes of femininity drawn from European sources, and that the job of a feminist criticism is to applaud those aspects of Canadian pioneer texts, historical romances, or early modernist novels that 'break through the artificiality in order to tell of the ways in which Canada changes [women's] ideas of themselves' (Buss, 'Canadian Women's Autobiography' 154). The best-known example of this approach is perhaps Margaret Atwood's characterization of *Roughing It in the Bush* as a schizophrenic text which incorporates two voices, one determined by the discourses of European decorum, religion, and art ('what you were supposed to feel') and one embodying the real Susanna who responds to the material facts of life in Upper Canada ('what you actually encountered when you got there').[2] *The Journals of Susanna Moodie*, like *The Embroidered Tent, The Pioneer Woman, Mapping Our Selves, Silenced Sextet,* and my own *A Different Point of View*,[3] rests on the premise that the role of language is to obscure or express already constituted feminine selves and so reproduce feminine experience in texts, bringing the real lives of women to witness in their fight for social equality. The mission of much feminist criticism of early Canadian texts has thus been founded upon a fundamental identification of the colloquial meaning of the word 'realistic' with the more specific, literary one: the former, for most readers, indicating a literal correspondence between the text and material reality; the latter indicating a literary technique which, for much of the last century, has been accepted as the only way of representing material reality.

The intellectual poverty of critical approaches which identify literary realism with the material reality of women's lives is now obvious to most readers of a theoretical bent; the work of Bina Freiwald, John Thurston, and others moves towards a more rigorous and theoretically informed criticism of early Canadian works. However, aside from Thurston, these forays have mainly consisted of scattered articles from critics whose major attention is focused elsewhere; published commentary on early Canadian writing often seems to be split between traditional historical scholarship and more theoretical approaches which represent a passing interest for critics whose main field is contemporary literature, and thus are often deficient in analysis of historical context. As Larry McDonald has pointed out, post-structuralist and postmodernist critics in Canada, while declaring the importance of historical specificity to the reading of texts, have to a large extent neglected the specific readings of historical texts which would validate their theoretical positioning;[4] in general, the acknowledgment of realism's ideological investments has prompted a turn towards contemporary experimental and non-realistic texts, rather than a more rigorous commentary on early works. This study attempts to address that lack by interrogating historical texts within their historical contexts to suggest how they function ideologically to produce and naturalize femininity.

This study defines femininity as the set of discursive practices which 'cite' the feminine gender ideal and which draw their legitimacy from the system of power which designates them as feminine. Drawing on Judith Butler's definition of gender as 'performative – that is, constituting the identity it is purported to be' (*Gender Trouble* 25), it demonstrates the way that practices which validate gender identification are predicated upon the assumption of a gendered 'inner self' which is supposed to be natural and existent, but whose existence is actually produced by the discourse of femininity. As Nancy Armstrong argues in *Desire and Domestic Fiction*, the wresting of power away from the aristocracy in eighteenth- and nineteenth-century England was accomplished through the idealization of a kind of woman whose feminine virtue was located beneath her surface; such women were valued, not for their familial connections, their sexual attributes, or their fortunes, but for the personal qualities of modesty, frugality, self-regulation, and intelligence which they brought to household management. Thus domestic ideology produces the illusion of an inner self whose essence is gender, and whose behaviour is constantly mobilized to validate the existence of that inner self. The establishment of a correspondence between the practice of femininity and its supposed essence as feminine inner self is mapped in this book through an analysis of the ideological work performed in texts by women and men.

In the texts to be considered, femininity will also be considered as practice within the discursive field of the literary text, which inscribes femininity in the textual decorum of genre, of content, and of stylistic convention.

As Armstrong points out, 'the domestic novel [was] the agent and product of a cultural change that attached gender to certain kinds of writing. Female writing – writing that was considered appropriate for or could be written by women – in fact designated itself as feminine' (28). Such self-consciously gendered texts, written in the supposedly feminine genres of the conduct book, the diary, and the novel, and claiming such feminine intentions as entertainment, gossip, and moral instruction, are the subjects of this study. These texts also practise femininity in their obsessive re-writing of the feminine self, a submission to the imperative to 'explain' in the course of reiteratively creating a feminine subject. The confession of 'what one is and what one does' (Foucault 60) constructs subjectivity in Western culture; therefore, texts represent themselves as progressively and definitively telling all about female experience. And this telling must be repeated over and over again, for 'heterosexual performativity is beset by an anxiety that it can never fully overcome, that its effort to become its own idealisations can never be finally or fully achieved' (Butler, *Bodies That Matter* 125). Gender can't be done once and be done with; femininity is a practice which must *be* practised, be repeated over and over again because it can never be done 'right,' can never materialize as a natural attribute of a material body. Because femininity can only be attributed to the fictional inner self whose existence it validates, we 'practis[e] femininity';[5] like Daphne Marlatt's Ana in *Ana Historic*, we continually try to get it right: 'Practice Makes Perfect, over and over.' And like the texts which it analyses, this study is itself an example of feminine practice.

The definition of femininity as practice does not imply a pre-existent self who chooses to act as a member of one or other gender: on the contrary, 'there is no gender identity behind the expressions of gender; ... [gender] is performatively constituted by the very "expressions" that are said to be its results' (Butler, *Gender Trouble* 25). While the ideology of femininity constructs an 'inner self,' a feminine essence which is supposed to be expressed by feminine practice, this study proceeds from the assumption that such an essence, though it is experienced as lived ideology, is a fiction. Thus, there is no pre-existing self prior to gender who can choose (or resist) it: '[a] "girl" ... is compelled to "cite" the norm in order to qualify and remain a viable subject. Femininity is thus not the product of a choice, but the forcible citation of a norm, one whose complex historicity is indissociable from relations of discipline, regulation, punishment. Indeed, there is no "one" who takes on a gender norm. On the contrary, this citation of the gender norm is necessary in order to qualify as a "one," to become viable as a "one," where subject formation is dependent on the

prior operation of legitimating gender norms' (*Bodies That Matter* 232).
Gender is thus an effect of the process of subjectivity, a process which
implies both active authority and passive submission: one becomes both
the subject of one's own story and subject to, subjected by, the limited categories offered by 'stories.' A distinction between the humanist self and
the subject will be used throughout this study, the former to indicate the
fictional self which the texts considered here struggle to materialize – a
unique individual who is marked by psychological consistency, memory,
emotion, and unity,[6] and by the specifically feminine virtues of self-control,
modesty, and frugality; who acts according to 'psychological motivation';
whose construction is the main theme of what Catherine Belsey calls classic
realism[7] – and the latter to indicate the subject who is a product of discourse and who is 'subjected' by entering into language.

Subjectivity is thus envisioned as both an enabling and a limiting process, and one which signals a kind of unavoidable complicity with patriarchy. The simple achievement of linguistic or narrative subjectivity is not
here envisioned as a desirable feminist goal,[8] for in responding to the 'hail'
of ideology one accepts, at some level, the category into which one is inter-
pellated. In order to achieve subjectivity at the most fundamental level,
consciousness of individual existence, one must accept one's relegation to
one or other gender, and thus become 'subjected' by its norms. For the
feminist woman, this process signals a basic ambivalence, for 'women
acquire a gendered identity by means of the very culture and ideology
which they seek to challenge' (Felski 27). Likewise, subjectivity as here conceived implies the impossibility of an easy escape from gender as constructed by symbolic language. One cannot simply choose, through an act
of will, to throw off gender identification, to become masculine or androgynous. Gender identification is a foundational structure in the creation of
the self, and thus integral to it; femininity is 'a norm one never chooses, a
norm that chooses us, but which we occupy, reverse, resignify to the extent
that the norm fails to determine us completely' (Butler, *Bodies* 126–7).

The occupation, reversal, and resignification of femininity is the focus
of the readings of specific texts which follow. For 'individuals are not
"subjects" wholly positioned by the system'; the contingencies of physical
life (including class and colonial status) as well as the ability to make (limited) choices produce fissures in ideology which allow individuals to
manoeuvre within the system that seeks to determine them (Durning 12).
While it is the 'role of ideology to suppress these contradictions in the
interests of the existing social formation ... their presence ensures that it
is always possible, with whatever difficulty, to identify them, to recognize

ideology for what it is, and to take an active part in transforming it by producing new meanings' (Belsey 45–6). These texts represent the 'work of words'[9] needed to resolve the ideological dilemmas which result from the disjunctions created by individual positioning within ideological structures; the result of such work is not simply the production of narrative closure for individual lives, but the redefinition of the ideological categories themselves. The readings of individual texts which follow seek to undo that closure and expose that redefinition, to do the work of Barthes's mythologist and reveal the role of history in the creation of what seems to be nature.

The concept of gender as a *condition* of speech radically revises the progressive narrative of women's liberation within which many literary texts by and about women have been interpreted. Rather than conceiving of gender as an artificial limitation upon a pre-existent self which may be thrown off almost at will by daring individual women,[10] this study views gender as a necessary part of the ideological system which brings individual selves into existence; Armstrong goes so far as to suggest that gender is the sole ideological foundation of the liberal concept of the individual in modern Western culture. Gender cannot therefore be escaped or thrown off; it cannot be considered as separate from the self which it constructs; it is the condition whereby individuals constitute themselves as autonomous, unique, and authoritative speakers.

In rejecting the traditional narrative of historical progress, this study attempts to follow an alternative concept of historical change which places renewed focus on texts and their historical contexts. This study is chronological, but this arrangement should not imply a narrative of progressive liberation; rather, it traces the mutations, over historical time, of an ideological system of subjection whose traces remain. Yet the persistence of the gender hierarchy does not imply that women are powerless, and this study does not suggest that women like myself – that is, white middle-class 'writing women' in cultures which derived from the British Empire – have ever been utterly powerless. To speak of feminine authority within the discourse of separate spheres may seem contradictory, for much feminist thinking in the past three decades has been premised upon showing how these categories oppressed and disenfranchised women. Yet, as Bronwen Wallace argued with vigour in her correspondence with Erin Mouré, the women of the past 'were *powerful* women *and* they were "under their husband's [*sic*] law" as well ... They used gossip, confession, anecdote, jokes – they used them ... to create a world in which the female was the metaphor for the universal' (McMaster 31). The female writers of the texts under consideration find a way of using the authority granted to them, an authority which was not granted to women of colour, women with less education or lower class status, or, for that matter, to classed or racialized men. By limiting this study to depictions of feminine practice among white middle-class women, I propose, in the words of Nancy Armstrong, to 'use my power as a woman of the dominant class and as middle-class intellectual to name what power I use as a form of power' (26), arguing that femininity was (and is) its own kind of power, however limited, and that women grasped that power in order to construct themselves and to be constructed as authoritative.

Much evidence can be cited to show that readers and writers in the nineteenth and early twentieth centuries thought that the changes in literary technique characterized as a progression from romance to realism were imitations or reflections of real-life advances gained for women. The lives of immigrant women as written out in the autobiographical narratives of the mid-nineteenth century were sufficiently different from those of their mothers to argue that immigration broke 'the cake of custom' (Bentley, 'Breaking the "Cake"' 93) which restricted women to their proper sphere. The liberation of the romance heroine from the necessity to be merely passive and decorative in the latter half of the nineteenth century seemed to reflect social advances in Canada which allowed women to attend university, and to acquire professions, independent incomes, and land. Sara Jeannette Duncan summed up this position in a much-quoted article in 1886: 'The novel of to-day is a reflection of our present social state. The women who enter into its composition are but intelligent agents in this reflection, and show themselves as they are, not as a false ideal would have them' ('Saunterings' 772). Showing women 'as they are' is a stated aim of Duncan's fiction, which regularly evokes the stereotypes of the 'old time heroine' or Kipling's memsahib in order to debunk them by contrast to female characters whose reality is signalled by their dissatisfaction with the roles offered to them by society and by their preoccupation with the material facts of their existence.

Yet these assumptions, shared by critics and writers alike (that realism represents an artistic advance over romantic or sentimental modes, that realistic depictions of women represent a political advance over romantic ones, and that Canada represents greater freedom for women than Europe), are challenged by the poststructuralist critique of language, which holds that a literary text can no more reproduce the real lives of women than Mary Pratt's painted fruit can be eaten. Literary realism, like the realist painting, is ideological, a discourse whose fundamental purpose is to erase the arbitrary relationship between the text and the material world[11] by creating the illusion that language is wholly referential. Mimesis in a literary text (as in a painting) can never be more than illusory: 'no narrative can "show" or "imitate" the story it tells. All it can do is tell it in a manner which is detailed, precise, "alive," and in that way give more or less the *illusion of mimesis* – which is the only narrative mimesis, for this single and sufficient reason: that narration, oral or written, is a fact of language, and language signifies without imitating' (Genette 164). The referential illusion which is the goal of realism is an effect of the process of signification; these texts tell us what is real by contrasting it to something else, which is designated 'not real' by the text itself. The choice of what to signify as real is ideological, and the reader's judgment as to the plausibility of character development, cause and effect, or closure, the correspondence of story to material reality, can only be dependent upon an agreement between the reader and the writer as to what reality is, an ideological consensus created by the dominant discourse of the text.

This study thus interrogates the ways in which the dominant discourses of these texts signify femininity, exposing the practices and the essential characteristics which they assign to women as naturally constituting their gendered selves. Focusing on works written in Canada between 1850 and 1940, it discusses the ways that works by Moodie, Traill, Leprohon, Dougall, Sime, Wood, McClung, and Ross justified this practice through the construction of a feminine inner self. The first five chapters analyse pioneer prose, historical romances, New Woman novels, and the politically engaged fiction of the suffrage movement, texts which self-consciously take Woman as their primary subject matter. The final chapter will read Sinclair Ross's *As for Me and My House* as an 'interrogative' realist text, showing how the novel signifies as real the psychological narrative of the feminine self developed by Freud and his predecessors.

The categorization of these texts as Canadian is in some senses arbitrary: the pioneer narratives were written and published before Canada existed as a political entity, and it might be argued that nationality is an unimportant distinction within what is a more generally Western (white, European, middle-class) concept of gendered subjectivity. However, as this study will demonstrate, the particularities of Canadian ideas about class mobility resulted in the redefinition of the feminine ideal. Canada itself was invested with meanings for immigrating groups,[12] and feminine gender practices developed in particular relation to these ideas, self-consciously accommodating and inscribing the deviation from European norms which the idea of Canada represented. As Canada became a self-conscious site of cultural difference from Europe, its own gender norms appeared in texts which address Canadian and foreign audiences from a self-consciously nativist point of view.

Femininity in a colonial society is a particularly contested discursive formation, drawing on a conservative belief in universal and continuous values which is contradicted by the liberal rhetoric of freedom characteristic of the New World. The supposed passivity and physical limitations of the nineteenth-century woman were contradicted by the necessity for active and physical labour on the Canadian bush farm. Femininity was reconstituted as consisting of the virtues which were instrumental to class mobility: primarily, a woman's ability to create domestic comfort and well-being wholly by her own labour and without expending any of the family income. Thus the 'self-made man' who owns his own land and in turn creates capital for further investment, turns out to be woman-made; the cash freed up for mortgage payments, and the unpaid labour which ran the family farm, were produced solely by women. In addition, the association of both Canada and women with the 'nature' side of the European nature/culture dyad makes the identification of femininity with nature a particularly important element of analysis, especially as psychological and biological science began to attribute instinctive or 'natural' sexual and maternal behaviour to the feminine self.

The political changes which characterized the rise of the domestic woman in England took a particular form in Canada. As the desirability of women came to be represented by their virtue and their ability to work, rather than their birth and aristocratic connections, a middle class united in its idealization of the specific kind of home which could be created by such a woman began to take shape. Virtue was relocated in the sensibilities and education of individuals, as evidenced by their manners and their personal integrity. This individualistic ideology was embraced with vigour in English Canada as providing justification for the changes in the class system created by the economic conditions of the new country. Catharine Parr Traill and Susanna Moodie declare in favour of a meritocratic system whereby individuals would claim influence over public policy by the force of their individual virtue; turn-of-the-century authors created an archetypal Canadian man who seemed oddly classless, happily competent at physical work yet educated and with refined tastes. The fiction that Canada is one big middle class arises from the desirability of the bourgeois domestic home and the ideology of the feminine self which supports it.

In an analysis of Catharine Parr Traill's *The Female Emigrant's Guide*, chapter 1 argues that Canadian conduct literature for emigrants operated as an ideological 'mending basket' which remade the connections between the economic behaviour demanded of emigrant women in Canada and the feminine inner self created by the ideology of the domestic woman. The ideology of the domestic woman held that her behaviour was governed by inner virtues such as modesty, frugality, devotion to duty, and self-control; in order to naturalize the new demands of Canadian life for physical labour, household chores, and the creation of products for sale, Canadian conduct literature reconnects these practices with the feminine inner self. Thus the central tautology of femininity is exposed: femininity consists in the performance of actions which have been previously gendered feminine, and the performance of such actions confirms the existence of a gendered inner self. Yet, in Canada, that inner self is mobilized to authorize the performance by women of new actions previously gendered masculine, and their performance provides new evidence of the existence of an unchanged, universal, and essentially feminine inner self. This reading of Canadian conduct literature challenges the often repeated statement that in immigrating to Canada, British 'gentlewomen' were offered the opportunity to escape from the restrictions of gender and to recover a more authentic self, or an androgynous ideal; rather, I argue that these women re-situated themselves within gender by using the concept of the gendered inner self to re-authorize their actions as feminine.

Chapter 2 explores the way that the concept of a gendered inner self can be mobilized to authorize speech, and more particularly the incursion of women authors into the masculine field of autobiographical writing. Susanna Moodie's autobiographical works 'Trifles from the Burthen of a Life,' *Flora Lyndsay*, *Roughing It in the Bush*, and *Life in the Clearings* reiterate a definition of the feminine self which foregrounds dutiful self-sacrifice, love of home and children, and submission to masculine authority. These works construct the career of a writer as only superficially inconsistent with feminine virtue, and proceed to justify autobiographical writing as a work of duty and submission, mobilizing the attributes of the feminine inner self as textual strategies to shape their departures from literary norms. In addition, they extend the concept of a virtuous inner self to justify and comment upon the changes in the British system of hierarchical government which were characteristic of Upper Canada.

Antoinette de Mirecourt, by Rosanna Leprohon, also mobilizes the concept of the feminine inner self to claim authority in a masculine realm: that of imperial-colonial politics. Leprohon's historical romance redefines the political issues of the relationship between British government and French-Canadian society as moral ones and therefore places them within the purview of feminine authority. Chapter 3 specifically analyses the romance plot of *Antoinette de Mirecourt*, arguing that by bracketing the romance and focusing on the realistic elements of the novel critics have repeated the gesture which domestic fiction structures: separation of the domestic world from the political, and the relegation of feminine authority to secondary status.

Chapter 4 analyses the way that New Woman fiction genders itself feminine by responding to the 'woman question.' The social situation which prompts the 'woman question' is dramatized in Jessie Sime's *Sister Woman* when a male listener demands of a female writer: 'State your grievance.' In responding to the question, New Woman novels create an anatomy of the interior life of Woman structured by the discourses of evolutionary and biological science, symbolically laying Woman bare to the gaze of authority. While the essentializing of women as biologically gendered grants women writers the authority to speak of their own experience, such speaking does not in itself grant power; instead, by constructing femininity according to the model of confession, New Woman novels reinsert themselves into the hierarchy of gender in a subordinate position.

Similarly, the practice of feminine 'self-expression' is figured as an ambivalent source of power in the fiction of Nellie McClung. Chapter 5 analyses the strategies employed in McClung's fiction and autobiography to claim authority within the public and political spheres of social policy, which rely upon a concept of the domestic woman as moral guardian and regulator of masculine desire. McClung's fiction generates a concept of 'the real' which it mobilizes to radically challenge stereotypical representations of domestic femininity; however, 'the real' of McClung's fiction generates a feminine nature and reifies a feminine self which finally reinforces rather than challenges gender ideology.

Chapter 6 challenges the essentialism which holds that female authors have privileged access to the ideology of the feminine by analysing the representation of the feminine inner self in Sinclair Ross's *As for Me and My House*. The chapter argues that the illusion of the inner self of the narrator is created by the evocation of two inconsistent cultural codes: those of the domestic woman and of the Freudian masculinity complex. Rather than being a strikingly 'real' representation whose referent is material feminine experience, Mrs Bentley is a formulaic representation of the undermining of the domestic ideal by the Freudian narrative of the feminine self whose inability to achieve access to masculine power deforms her social relationships. *As for Me and My House* demonstrates the way that the scientific construction of the feminine inner self as sexual, often represented by critics as a political advance for women, may be mobilized to reinforce women's subjection by creating them as unstable and untruthful.

In analysing these works as ideological, this study leaves aside the question of their literary value according to modernist aesthetic standards. Following a methodology which has been associated with the discipline of cultural studies, this study assumes that such standards of evaluation are themselves primarily ideological[13] and that 'a literary reputation could never be anything but a political matter' (Tompkins, *Sensational Designs* 4). While traditional critics of writers such as Traill, Moodie, Leprohon, Wood, Sime, Dougall, McClung, and Ross have mobilized the concept of literary value defensively in order to justify their inclusion in a canon of publication and academic criticism, this study assumes that the texts under consideration are of interest because they do 'a certain kind of cultural work within a specific historical situation ... expressing and shaping the social context that produced them' (ibid. 200). Rather than making a case for their inclusion within a canon of Canadian Literature on the grounds of their unity and complexity, I present them merely as 'examples of the way a culture thinks about itself' (ibid. xi) and valuable for that reason.[14]

1

The Female Emigrant's Guide
as the Mending Basket of Domestic Ideology

Abundant commentary on appropriate feminine behaviour in Catharine Parr Traill's *Female Emigrant's Guide* suggests the rupture in the ideology of femininity which was caused by immigration to Upper Canada. It was, as Traill says, 'a matter of surprize' to middle-class emigrants that their new lives demanded that women contribute economically to the welfare of their families, producing such items as soap, bread, butter, preserves, vegetables, and sugar for household use, or worse, labouring in the fields, chopping, underbrushing, ploughing, and reaping. The commentary which accompanies the practical instructions in the *Guide* suggests that, as products of a middle-class society in which women's social roles as consumers, moral guardians, and objects of exchange between men were strictly prescribed, Traill and her contemporaries found it difficult to justify their new social and economic role as labourers and producers of goods for home consumption or for sale. While life on a farm in Canada clearly offered greater scope for independent action than their previous lives in England, writers of pioneer texts like Traill and her sister Susanna Moodie did not embrace this independence as easily or wholeheartedly as a simple opposition between European confinement and Canadian freedom would suggest.

Critics have often viewed pioneer women's engagement in duties and pastimes previously understood to be masculine, and their putting aside of the standards of dress and respectability demanded in England, as evidence of a personal choice to 'escape from the shackles of gender-stereotyping into a wide-open, freely chosen world of individual responses and behaviour' (Fowler, *ET* 10). Clara Thomas suggests that Traill knew 'from experience that in pioneer life the roles of male and female cannot be sharply defined' and emphasized that in immigration to Canada, individuals must be able to assume the role appropriate to the opposite sex (Introduction, *Canadian Settler's Guide* x). These approaches were common from the late 1960s to the 1980s, but more recent critics also generally accept the premise that gender can be 'escaped' or chosen. David Bentley argues that the New World offered women 'choices' on a scale of femininity between the archetypes of the 'Madonna' and the 'Hercules,' 'options that could be chosen fairly straightforwardly or combined in complex, exciting, and genuinely liberating ways' ('Breaking the "Cake"' 100–1). For Bentley, women who performed 'such traditionally masculine labours as ploughing, sowing, and harvesting, blurred the conventional distinctions between the sexes' (95–6) or even behaved like men (107) and in so doing 'forged in their lives and in their writings a new role model for Canadian women ... to create and embody the gender-blurring *topos* of the female Crusoe' (96). Yet, he argues, such women felt the need to 'remain feminine in the conventional terms of their day' (96), and he characterizes the result as a 'tension between the "masculine" and the "feminine," the necessary and the conventional' (96). Likewise, Elizabeth Thompson is bound by the dualisms suggested by Margaret Atwood in *The Journals of Susanna Moodie,* of masculine/feminine, necessity/convention, reality/ideality, New World/Old World. She argues that pioneer women were 'forced to ... redefine their feminine role' (Thompson 4) and that this redefinition led to a new 'character type' who contradictorily held to conventional ideas of feminine behaviour and particularly class behaviour, while performing the feats of masculine endeavour required by 'reality.' Thompson argues that Traill expressed this dichotomy by writing realistic prose tempered by 'a strong moral bias and an obvious tendency to colour real events with a cheerful idealism' (5).

For both Bentley and Thompson, Traill's use of the figure of the 'Crusoe' in her novel *Canadian Crusoes* and in *The Backwoods of Canada* represents a consciously masculine ideal which, they argue, shapes the role of women in the New World. However, while the twentieth century is apt to think of *Crusoe* as a specifically masculine novel of adventure and exploration, the nineteenth did not necessarily agree: Nancy Armstrong notes that *Robinson Crusoe* was one of the novels specifically recommended for the education of girls (and *not* boys) in Maria Edgeworth's *Practical Education* (1801). Armstrong suggests that Crusoe was an essentially domestic figure because he created 'a totally self-enclosed and functional domain where money did not really matter' (16). Indeed, the main actions in the book are the feminine ones of arranging household concerns, enduring hardship in the acceptance of God's will, and educating the heathen.

When compared with Defoe's nominally female heroes like Moll Flanders or Roxana, Crusoe appears much 'more female' (16). Thus Traill's references to Crusoe as a model for feminine behaviour need not be seen as the expression of a desire to become masculine, but rather to domesticate both men and women.

Thus critical approaches to pioneer women's writing rest on several assumptions that seem problematic. They assume that the material author's personality, while partially obscured by literary discourses, is available in the autobiographical text. They assume a degree of agency which is tautological in the formation of the self, and suggest that femininity is merely an aspect of personality which varies individually. In arguing for a kind of 'literary heroinism' whereby women are enabled to free themselves from femininity by an act of will, or even make themselves masculine, they assume that for Traill and other pioneer women, gender is merely conventional; that such women, as essential selves which pre-exist gender, could choose not only to perform masculine tasks, but to *be* masculine; that femininity was primarily a systematic restriction upon the self which any rational person would instantly discard, given the chance.[1] However, if gender is seen as a system for the production of the self within language and a necessary condition of selfhood, Traill could no more choose to discard it than she could discard her sanity.

Pioneer conduct literature[2] held the ideological tenet that femininity is an absolute value which cannot be changed simply by a change in geographical location. When the settlement of British North America began in earnest around 1820, the British immigrants to Upper and Lower Canada who joined the English-speaking Loyalists and their descendants to create what would become a sense of distinctive nationhood, imported their ideas about femininity, as on most topics, from England. The educated Loyalist culture of the East Coast took its cultural lead from England, and the generation that immigrated to the Canadas during 1820–40 grew up in England, Ireland, and Scotland, and so brought their ideas with them. In both cases, their ideas on the nature of woman and the expression of that nature by conduct were formed by late eighteenth- and early nineteenth-century British culture. In her conduct book *Letters to a Young Lady on Leaving School and Entering the World* (1855), New Brunswick author Sarah French specifically rejects the tenet that standards of behaviour for women may vary by culture: 'pert forwardness of manner seems more peculiar to this side of the Atlantic; but right and wrong are of no country, or rather they belong to all and the same rule of duty: the same standard of correctness of behavior pertains to all places and people' (67). In the period from 1820 to 1870, the idea that standards of behaviour might change, or had changed, when they crossed the Atlantic was strongly resisted in conduct books and in fictional and autobiographical narrative. While Traill was inclined to celebrate her escape from 'Mrs Grundy'[3] in the backwoods of Canada, she did so by representing social authority by a stereotype of excessive conformity; thus her departures from strict standards of social behaviour appear as moderate and rational adaptations to circumstance, rather than uniquely Canadian expressions of freedom.

The ideal of feminine behaviour upon which Traill and her contemporaries modelled their sense of self derived from the culture of the eighteenth and nineteenth centuries in England. As industrial capitalism became the dominant mode of production in England, newly rich families wanted to add to their prestige and social position by marrying into landed families. As landed families became increasingly land-poor, they in turn looked to alliances through marriage with newly rich industrial families to save their family estates. Middle-class women performed an important economic function in these transactions and came to accept 'a definition of "female nature" that was derived from a social role' (Poovey 15), that is, from the role of counter in family attempts to gain social status. If women were to be used as embodiments of exchange value by men in attempts to gain important social and financial connections, 'women's behaviour must significantly differ from that of men, who express their own wishes, make their own choices' (Poovey 4). 'Until the nineteenth century, women were viewed as a lesser version of men, but a replica nevertheless' (Mitchinson, *The Nature* 35); during the nineteenth century, thinkers elaborated on the divergent development of men and women in order to justify their differing social roles. Primarily, women were defined as unable to make decisions in the public world and as lacking in personal desire – for this would threaten the project of capital acquisition by the law of primogeniture. Self-effacement and strict chastity, evidenced not only by sexual modesty but by piety and rigid control over all passions including anger and simple enjoyment, were the first requisites of feminine behaviour, for 'the surest safeguard against overindulgence was not to allow or admit to appetites of any kind. Thus women were encouraged to display no vanity, no passion, no assertive "self" at all. In keeping with this design, even genuinely talented women were urged to avoid all behaviour that would call attention to themselves' (Poovey 21).

Yet the nineteenth-century ideology of femininity was not a simple restriction upon free action. Rather, it created a sphere of discourse in which women were granted authority, and generated a concept of the inner self which valued women for their personal qualities rather than their sexual attributes or their fortunes.[4] The specific form of the historical category of the feminine which provides authority in nineteenth-century Canada was constituted by submission to the 'sexual contract.' Domestic fiction used the concept of the contract to create an analogy between political choices made in the public sphere and personal choices made in the domestic sphere. Rousseau's 'social contract' explains society by arguing that the 'individual ... volunteer[s] to curb his acquisitive appetite so that he might secure his property and live in peace with others' (Armstrong 31), thus leaving himself free for the greater goals of 'self-perfection' (Armstrong 32). The fiction of a voluntary submission to power in order to gain specified benefits is self-contradictory, implying both the existence of a pre-social subject who can choose to enter a contract, as well as a pre-existing society with which to contract. However, novels 'translated the social contract into a sexual exchange' (Armstrong 38) by creating the fiction of a 'sexual contract' of marriage. 'A sexual exchange – where he fights with competing members of his species for her, and she in return domesticates him ... differentiates individuals within a given species according, first and foremost, to gender. It is on this basis that Mill and Darwin exempt women from political relations and detach domestic life, by definition, from the competitive practices that are supposed to characterize men' (Armstrong 40). According to the sexual contract, men protect women in return for their domestication: 'the female relinquishes political control to the male in order to acquire exclusive authority over domestic life, emotions, taste and morality' (quoted in Armstrong 41). While it is clear that 'social applications of this model' were and continue to be severe restrictions on women's lives, the model 'purports to empower them' (Armstrong 40) by giving them exclusive control over the domestic sphere. This sphere was created in the newly popular genre of conduct books for women, which joined together aspects of the ideal woman as envisioned by earlier courtesy literature, devotional books, and practical handbooks on household management to create an ideal woman who was a sensible, modest, and tasteful consumer, rather than an extravagantly conspicuous (and expensive) object of display. The 'domestic ideal' held that the most desirable women were not simply passive, 'lack[ing] the competitive desires and worldly ambitions that ... belonged – as if by some natural principle – to the male' (Armstrong 59), but were also endowed with the positive attributes necessary to become active, knowledgeable, and dutiful managers of their husbands' homes. The household came to represent the interior life of the woman rather than the income of her husband, and conduct literature focused on the aspects of household management – relations with servants, planning of meals and entertainments, or supervision of children – which would demonstrate the 'qualities of the desirable woman – her discretion, modesty and frugality' (Armstrong 73).

Foremost among these qualities was 'self-regulation' or self-control, the containment and regulation of desire. The domestic woman, using practical sense, taste, and intelligence, was able to regulate her household expenses by regulating her own desires; the result was the creation of a comfortable and pleasant household whose expenses did not deplete her husband's capital. Similarly, these qualities allowed the domestic woman to regulate the behaviour of men, whose otherwise uncontained energies were a threat to civil and domestic order. From this role, it followed that women were morally superior to men and that the essence of feminine gender consisted of women's ability to control and regulate moral behaviour both inside and outside the home. Conspicuous consumption in order to display one's place in a social hierarchy became unfashionable; what took its place was the 'subordination of money to a higher standard of value.' This standard of value, represented by the supposed moral virtues of the domestic woman, 'distinguished the ideal household from family life both at the top and at the bottom of the social ladder' (Armstrong 82). The new household 'provided a common ideal for individuals who would otherwise see themselves in competition or else without any relationship at all' (19) and so 'enabled a coherent idea of the middle class to take shape' (Armstrong 63).[5]

The domestic ideal generates a concept of the inner self by locating femininity underneath the surface of the physical body, and making it invisible to the casual observer.[6] Conduct books held that 'a woman was deficient in female qualities if she, like the aristocratic woman ... aimed at putting the body on display' (Armstrong 75) or if, like the labouring woman, she was valued merely for her performance of physical duties. 'By implying that the essence of the woman lay inside or underneath her surface, the invention of depths in the self entailed making the material body of the woman appear superficial' (76), and the qualities of an ideal mate came to be judged by a standard created by 'the judicious cultivation of the female understanding' (Maria Edgeworth, cited in Fowler, *ET* 59) and the ability to 'reason, and reflect, and feel, and judge, and discourse, and discriminate' (Hannah More, cited in Fowler, *ET* 59). Gender is no longer confirmed by the simple inspection of the physical body recommended in More's *Utopia*, but becomes a complex question of relating outward behaviour to supposed inner qualities. The concept of gender as inner self eventuated in a system whereby the performance of certain prescribed duties and the miming of certain prescribed emotional states are necessary to 'prove' the existence of a valid gendered inner self. If the performance of these duties becomes impossible, or the circumstances which allow appropriate emotional display are changed, new ways to make the connection between a supposed interior life and outward behaviour must be created, or gender divisions (and so personal identity) become unstable.

Texts produced by immigrants who settled in New Brunswick or in the back townships of Ontario practise the conventional femininity of their European antecedents by conforming to the literary genres which were held to be appropriate to women. Collections of letters describing the process of emigration, such as Traill's *The Backwoods of Canada*, demonstrate the close emotional ties between family members and love of home which characterize the feminine inner self. In addition, such texts gender themselves feminine by providing the moral guidance of an exemplary life lived under difficult conditions. *The Female Emigrant's Guide* conforms to the decorum of genre by addressing itself primarily to female readers and by claiming an authority based upon its conformity to the domestic stereotype: a review in the *Irish Canadian* commended the author as a 'Christian lady' whose work 'cannot fail, if duly heeded, to encourage, guide and instruct' (5 April 1865, 5). Containing diverse kinds of information including recipes, instructions on how to make household furniture and graft fruit trees, and advice on coping with the emotional demands of leaving home and submitting to the will of God, *The Female Emigrant's Guide* inherits its generic conventions from British conduct books which combined the generic attributes of devotional literature, courtesy books, and domestic economies.

But while it conforms to the decorum of genre, *The Female Emigrant's Guide* also shows how conventional gender divisions were destabilized by emigration. In its account of the circumstances of life in the backwoods, it details women's performance of tasks which would be inappropriate and unfeminine in England, such as manual labour and the creation of products for sale outside the home.[7] The justification of such tasks in terms of the ideology of domesticity is iterated and reiterated in the *Guide*, and the femininity of manual and productive labour asserted with obsessive vigour. Because femininity can never materialize as an attribute of a physical body or become apparent to the naked eye, the *Guide* must make and remake the relationship between the feminine practice it recommends and the feminine inner self that such practice validates. Books such as *The Female Emigrant's Guide* are not simply compilations of useful facts; they are conduct literature, the ideological mending basket of the female emigrant, the place where the femininity of these new tasks was established by their linkage to the essentially feminine inner self of the domestic woman.[8]

The British model of middle-class femininity was ruptured for the female emigrant by the necessity of manual labour, the physical danger and hardship of the new life, and the inability to rely upon men for protection and help. While the domestic woman in Britain expressed her nature by her intelligent supervision of housework and her tasteful planning of meals and decor, the ideology of domesticity continued to relegate actual physical labour to the lower-class domestic, who was consequently masculinized by its performance (Armstrong 20): 'though conduct books represented aristocratic behaviour as the very antithesis of the domestic woman, they never once exalted labour' (Armstrong 78). 'Agrarian and artisan forms of labour were considered unfeminine' (68) in British conduct books for women, and while such books adopted many of the elements of the earlier domestic economies, they 'ceased to provide advice for the care of livestock or the concoction of medicinal cures' (Armstrong 67), deeming such work outside the home to be outside the scope of the domestic woman. The British reception of works about life in Canada by Moodie and Traill tends to confirm that the manual labour expected of a settler's wife was considered an unreasonable and unnatural demand, which could only be fulfilled by extraordinary strength and persistence. An anonymous review in *Blackwoods* exhorted Moodie's readers, the 'Ladies of England, deftly embroidering in carpeted saloon, gracefully bending over easel or harp, pressing with nimble finger, your piano's ivory,' to 'look forth into the desert at a sister's sufferings!' In the review, Moodie appears unclassed as well as ungendered, 'work[ing] in the rugged and inclement wilderness, harder than the meanest of the domestics, whom, in her own country, she was used to command' ('Forest Life' 355). The *Athenaeum* reviewer of *Roughing It* notes that Moodie 'bent herself womanfully to field work when necessity required,' emphasizing by his punning turn on 'manfully' the inappropriateness of field work to his view of feminine gender (28 Feb. 1852, 247). Members of the Strickland family left behind in England were mortified by the book, which exposed both poverty and unfeminine behaviour to public view.[9] A review of *The Backwoods of Canada* in the *Athenaeum* repeated Traill's own argument that the 'delicately nurtured' woman needs to seek 'compensation for the difficulties and rudenesses of an emigrant's lot' in the beauty of nature (20 Feb. 1836, 138). While the Canadian notices of *The Female Emigrant's Guide*, in contrast, accept the inevitability of work for women and praise the 'practical' advice offered in the book, paradoxically they placed these sentiments alongside reprinted British articles that extolled women's fragility.[10]

In order to present physical labour as a feminine practice in the New World, the *Guide* undertakes the ideological task of de-classing labour. Because domesticity held that by the performance of physical labour the bodies of lower-class women were rendered less feminine, the *Guide* re-establishes the femininity of physical labour by linking it to the virtues of the feminine inner self such as duty, modesty, frugality, and self-regulation. *The Female Emigrant's Guide* confronts this issue explicitly by addressing readers' fears of being de-classed by physical labour. The text recounts example after example of 'officers' wives' and gentlewomen whose participation in physical tasks has not de-classed them: 'In the early years of our infant settlement on the banks of the Otonabee river, above the town of Peterboro', all the ladies worked in their gardens ... They felt this work as no disgrace to them, but took pride and pleasure in the success of their labours' (69). Indoors, knitting 'must form one of the occupations of the females of the higher or more educated class ... To the mind of the well-regulated female, there is no disgrace in so feminine an occupation: ... and indeed [she] would be considered as a very useless and foolish person, if she despised that which every one here practises' (179). Anecdotes of gentlewomen 'who have not only planted and hoed the corn, but have also harvested it' (115) are interspersed with suggestions that those who are too nice to descend to such work are deficient in their duty towards their families.

Attendance to duty is one of the most important aspects of the domestic woman. Nineteenth-century conduct literature condemned intellectual pursuits and even the religious studies characteristic of seventeenth- and eighteenth-century aristocratic women because they seemed to be a retreat from duty in the world (Armstrong 68), and Traill condemns the common stereotype of the prideful and self-absorbed aristocratic woman to justify not only physical labour in trying circumstances but the acquisition of ordinary household skills. 'Instead of suffering a false pride to stand in their way of acquiring practical household knowledge, let it be their pride – their noble, honest pride – to fit themselves for the state which they will be called upon to fill – a part in the active drama of life' (16). The learning of skills like bread-making, gardening, butter- and cheese-making, is offered by the *Guide* as no more than putting 'in practice that which they learned to repeat with their lips in childhood as a portion of the catechism, "To do my duty in that state of life, unto which it may please God to call me"' (16).[11]

The *Guide* does condemn much heavy work in the backwoods as unsuitable for women, largely because of the weakness of their bodies. It counts sugar-making as 'rough work, and fitter for men,' and suggests that though women have been known to take part in 'underbrushing, and even helping to lay up and burn a fallow,' the work 'was unfit for them' (141). Yet the *Guide* suggests that the performance of such work may be seen to validate feminine gender by demonstrating the ability of the gendered inner self to overcome the weakness of the female body, as in the following comments: 'I have marked with astonishment and admiration acts of female heroism, for such it may be termed in women whose former habits of life had exempted them from any kind of laborious work, urged by some unforeseen exigency, perform tasks from which many men would have shrunk. Sometimes aroused by the indolence and inactivity of their husbands or sons, they have resolutely set their own shoulders to the wheel, and borne the burden with unshrinking perseverance unaided; forming a bright example to all around them, and showing what can be done when the mind is capable of overcoming the weakness of the body' (36–7). The female body is at its most feminine when subordinated to the virtues of the gendered inner self; this argument nullifies the suggestion that physical labour, by focusing on the body, might masculinize the domestic woman. In addition, Traill argues that in later years these examples of the subordination of the female body to feminine duty will serve to inculcate virtue in children (116), again linking the performance of physical tasks to the appropriate feminine practice of the moral education of children. The examples she cites of women who preserve their families from fire or harvest crops alone while nursing ill husbands are heroines not because they act beyond the expectations of femininity, or because they throw off femininity in order to act as individuals; on the contrary, they are heroines because they manage to act completely in accord with femininity and its discipline of self-denial and self-sacrifice. For Traill, 'the greatest heroine in life is she who knowing her duty, resolves not only to do it, but to do it to the best of her abilities, with heart and mind bent upon the work' (16).

The *Guide* never wavers from the division of labour which the ideology of domesticity creates; the role of men in the home is specifically constructed as absent.[12] Men may be called upon to dig gardens or plant orchards, to make attractive fences or construct poultry yards; men should 'do all they can to make the house as convenient as circumstances will admit' (198) by adding verandas to log houses and digging convenient cellars or ice houses. But the *Guide* makes it clear that their assistance cannot be counted on. Besides the possibility of their falling ill or becoming injured, the fact is that they have their own work to do, which is out-of-doors and concerned with capital accumulation and long-term prosperity: 'If the men will not devote a portion of time to the cultivation of the garden, and orchard, the women must, or else forego all the comfort that they would otherwise enjoy' (68). While the domestic woman in Britain gave orders within a domestic sphere defined by her authoritative knowledge, the Canadian housewife transforms that sphere into a scene of action and responsibility. But that scene is defined no more or less for the Canadian by the same ideology of domesticity.

Another gap in the ideology of domesticity is opened up by emigration itself. A defining element of the feminine inner self generated by domesticity is love of home, expressed as an integral emotional attachment to both the physical space of home and to the family members associated with it. By this criterion, the woman who is capable of successfully emigrating is by definition absolutely unfeminine. *The Female Emigrant's Guide* consequently addresses the issue of 'love of home' as a central one, not only because its readers see themselves as what Marian Fowler calls 'Hartshorn-and-Handkerchief Heroines' (Fowler, *ET* 7), but because removal of the domestic woman from home represents a major ideological contradiction. In its description of women's feelings upon leaving home, the *Guide* specifies that it is the 'nature' of women 'to love home and to cling to all home ties and associations,' and that truly feminine women 'cannot be torn from that spot that is the little centre of joy and peace and comfort to her, without many painful regrets' (25). As part of its description of the emigrant woman as woman, the text produces the necessity of regrets, tears, and depression, 'for in this attachment to home lies much of her [a woman's] charm as a wife and mother in his [her husband's] eyes' (26).[13] The *Guide* suggests that this essential feminine virtue may be mitigated by placing it under the sway of maternal feelings, as hopes for the 'future welfare of their children' (16) must be the 'main-spring that urges them to make the sacrifice' (17); love of home may also be subordinated to duty by producing 'an earnest endeavour to render her new dwelling equally charming' (26) as the old home. Yet, as such love is an essential quality of the feminine inner self, it can never be overcome: 'the remembrance of [home] never leaves her; it is graven on her heart' (25).

Traill chooses to claim personal authority in discussing this issue, for it is one which is particularly vexed; she gains authority as a writer by identifying herself within the category of the feminine from which, by her emigration, she has been exiled. She reclaims her enunciatory position thus: 'I write from my own experience. I too have felt all the painful regrets incidental to a long separation from my native land and my beloved early home. I have experienced all that you who read this book can ever feel, and perhaps far more than you will ever have cause for feeling' (28). This emphasis on the 'truth and authenticity' which the 'recording "I"' (Thurston, 'Ideologies of the I' 25) guarantees is common to all pioneer narratives of early Canada, but has special significance for the female writer. For the choice to speak authoritatively as 'I' in this instance has the effect of re-situating the author's own unfeminine act of emigration within the set of practices authorizing the feminine inner self.

Conduct literature of the eighteenth and nineteenth centuries in England succeeded in creating a new kind of desirable woman. The very definition of a desirable female 'hinged upon an education in frugal domestic practices. She was supposed to complement [her husband's] role as an earner and producer with hers as a wise spender and tasteful consumer' (Armstrong 59). New World conduct literature such as *The Female Emigrant's Guide* created a different sort of desirable woman, the complement of her male partner, who needed a productive labourer as well as a domestic manager: 'Every young woman is prized in this country according to her usefulness; and a thriving young settler will rather marry a clever, industrious girl, who has the reputation for being a good spinner and knitter, than one who has nothing but a pretty face to recommend her. This is at it should be' (178). While the creation of the domestic ideal in England had the effect of consolidating and producing a middle class which was united in its pursuit of a specific form of household, in Canada this domestic ideal, appropriately worked to patch over the gaps made apparent in its transplantation, also produced a united middle class. The process whereby the common striving towards the achievement of the domestic ideal unified social groups was forwarded by the de-classing of domestic labour in Canada and its representation as a necessary stage in the reproduction of capital, in the form of lands, investments, and financial independence. In Canada, feminine frugality is aimed towards 'not expending her husband's means' (26) in domestic expenses. By producing almost every item of household use – soap, clothes, furniture, pillows, pies, and sugar – from the produce of the farm, women were expected to provide comfortable living conditions, nourishing meals, and unpaid farm workers (in the form of children) while allowing all available cash to be accumulated for investment in land title and improvement.[14] 'Everything that is done in the house by the hands of the family, is so much saved or so much earned towards the paying for the land or building houses and barns, buying stock or carrying on the necessary improvements on the place: the sooner this great object is accomplished, the sooner will the settler and his family realize the comfort of feeling themselves independent' (14–15). The *Guide* represents feminine labour as common to households of all classes and all ethnic backgrounds in the backwoods, where servants are often unavailable and household goods cannot be purchased. In addition, the *Guide* represents such living conditions as a stage of life common to all emigrants which will lead to economic prosperity, ownership of valuable land, and high-status education and professional occupations or even political office for children, if feminine management is properly applied. Thus feminine self-control is the essential quality for the reproduction of the so-called 'self-made man' who rises from poverty to prosperity, and central to the creation of the middle class in Canada. As Susan Jackel has noted, 'One could argue that domestication, not conquest, is the message spelled out by peace, order and good government' (99).

Traill's modest commendations of useful toil and frugal domestic habits, her applause of the lack of social affectation in the bush, and her condemnations of aristocratic or conspicuous forms of dress are not in themselves uniquely Canadian feminine practice.[15] Nor are they the result of the interaction between her unique 'self' and her experience in the real world. Instead, they represent the ideological work necessary to mend the gap between inner self and outward practice which emigration opened up for nineteenth-century British women. By showing the ways in which the new practices required of a desirable woman in pioneer British North America may be understood to confirm the existence of a gendered inner self, *The Female Emigrant's Guide* does the work necessary to maintain the enunciatory position from which women claimed the authority to speak in colonial British cultures. In this way, Traill's book is vitally linked to the more obviously literary and autobiographical works such as Susanna Moodie's *Roughing It in the Bush*, which claim gender as authority to speak within traditionally masculine literary genres.

2

The Broken Mirror of Domestic Ideology: Femininity as Textual Practice in Susanna Moodie's Autobiographical Works

'The Broken Mirror, a True Tale,' by Susanna Moodie (published in the *Literary Garland* in 1843), takes its name from an anecdote which is rich in symbolic associations. A heartbroken emigrant mother rescues an elaborate Italian mirror from the sale of her family possessions. Initially, the mirror seems to be the symbol of a stubborn attachment to her previous station in life, and she is ridiculed by her neighbours and advisors for refusing to accept the reality of her poverty. However, her decision is justified as the mirror becomes the means of re-establishing her family after their immigration to South Africa: though the mirror shatters on the voyage, the shards are sold to native Africans and the proceeds used to buy a comfortable home. The mirror is a traditional symbol of femininity, associated with vanity and with the creation of a self dependent upon the gaze of others. Its shattering suggests the rupture in the ideology of the feminine which results from the voyage, both mental and physical, from Briton to colonist.[1] In this story, as in *Roughing It in the Bush* and Moodie's other autobiographical works, the Old World mirror of femininity initially seems unsuited to life in the New World, and those who cling to it are ridiculed. However, though Old World ideology is broken by the voyage, its pieces, reorganized and reconceived, form the basis of the self in the New World.

Like *The Female Emigrant's Guide*, *Roughing It in the Bush* inscribes the feminine according to the domestic ideal of nineteenth-century England. Moodie's autobiographical works express a need to naturalize gender in the bodies of women through reiterative accounts of gendered qualities such as homesickness, endurance, self-denial, self-control, and nurturance and love of children. By invoking the values associated with domesticity, they justify feminine authorship; by simultaneously invoking the characteristics of a supposed feminine inner self and inscribing them as structural principles, the texts gender themselves and claim the authority of feminine subjectivity to assert an autobiographical self. 'Trifles from the Burthen of a Life,'[2] *Flora Lyndsay*, *Roughing It in the Bush*, and *Life in the Clearings* mobilize the domestic ideal to both justify and structure the unconventional appearance of a feminine textual self in the public realm of the autobiographical text, and show how the practice of writing for publication can be understood to validate the existence of a feminine inner self.

In *Letters to a Young Lady on Leaving School and Entering the World*, Sarah French formulates the opposition between domestic femininity and the practice of writing for publication which governs Moodie's self-presentation in all of her autobiographical works: 'if you ever think to become a wife, never venture in the paths of literature: a woman who seeks notoriety in them is rarely calculated for the quiet detail of domestic duty. She has entered the public arena, and must there seek her happiness' (49). According to domestic ideology, the woman who prides herself upon her achievements as a writer loses the limited authority granted her by her interpellation as feminine and is in danger of being judged unwomanly. *Roughing It in the Bush* reports that its narrator had become well known in the Cobourg area as the 'woman that writes,' an object of embarrassing comments in the popular press and of gossip and speculation among the townspeople. Advised by two neighbours to 'lay by the pen, and betake [her]self to some more useful employment,' such as making shirts for her husband, or cleaning house, she protests: 'These remarks were completely gratuitous, and called forth by no observations of mine; for I tried to conceal my blue stockings beneath the long conventional robes of the tamest commonplace, hoping to cover the faintest tinge of the objectionable colour ...' The text continues: 'Anxious not to offend them, I tried to avoid all literary subjects,' and became 'more diligent in cultivating every branch of domestic usefulness' – in an attempt to reify the domestic 'inner self' that writing seemed to contradict (*RI* 202).[3]

As a young woman, Susanna Strickland had written in a letter to Mary Russell Mitford that 'a desire for fame appears to me almost inseparable from an author' (quoted in Shields, 3). Yet her letters, poems, and prose reveal from her youth onward her growing awareness that the 'woman that writes' for fame or for personal satisfaction transgresses the common idea of the feminine 'self.' The lyric poetry she published in *Enthusiasm; and Other Poems* (1831) gives evidence of perhaps unconscious anxiety about whether lyric expression of personality is consistent with femininity. The title poem of her collection is addressed to the emotion which is alike the inspiration of religious conversion and of poetry; but the speaker consistently refers to those heroes and poets moved by the spirit as 'he'; in the companion piece, 'Fame,' and the dialogue 'Fancy and the Poet,' the poet is also male. Susanna Strickland seems to have concluded that lyric poetry is not feminine; Susanna Moodie's letters concerning her marriage and the birth of her first daughter, Kate, state her intention to give up the public voice of poetry altogether in favour of the domestic virtues of wife and mother. Like the conduct books of the period, the letters place writing for publication among the despised 'accomplishments' of worldly husband-hunters, and imply that for a woman, domestic happiness is inconsistent with a career as a writer. In a letter to her poet friend James Bird, she writes: 'My blue stockings, since I became a wife, have turned so pale that I think they will become quite white ... [I] now find, that the noble art of housewifery is more to be desired than all the accomplishments, which are to be retailed by the literary and fashionable damsels' (*Letters of a Lifetime* 61). To his wife, Emma Bird, six months later, Susanna Moodie reiterates, 'I have quarrelled with rhymes ever since I found out how much happier we can be without them. Domestic comfort is worth all the literary fame that ever pu[lled] a youthful Bard onto the pinnacle of pub[lic] notice' (*Letters of a Lifetime* 65).[4]

Given the opposition between writing and femininity created by domestic ideology, a major interest in Moodie's fiction is femininity, how one achieves it and what it is composed of. *Flora Lyndsay,* 'Trifles from the Burthen of a Life,' *Roughing It,* and *Life in the Clearings* obsessively return to the definition of a supposed feminine nature and compulsively gender their protagonists, often in contrast to other, insufficiently gendered characters. The characteristics of feminine nature inscribed in these texts are similar to those delineated in *The Female Emigrant's Guide*: modesty, self-sacrifice, love of children, self-control. The books assert that women are unique in their ability to love children (see, for example, *Flora Lyndsay* 5, *Life in the Clearings* 46); that their interests are identical to their children's (*Flora Lyndsay* 83); and that they are made to be mothers (*Flora Lyndsay* 72). Because they put the welfare of their children first, they are ruled by self-control and self-sacrifice (*RI* 194), and thus are able to govern themselves and provide for their households with 'economy and good management' (*Flora Lyndsay* 11). These characteristics of the feminine 'inner self' are often, but not always, externalized as physical beauty; they are always manifest in a gentle and modest manner, 'patient endurance of suffering and privation' (*Flora Lyndsay* 95),[5] and submission to the authority of parent and husband.

Moodie's autobiographical works particularly stress two aspects of feminine nature related to the project of emigration: love of home and submission to authority. Like *The Female Emigrant's Guide, Roughing It in the Bush* and *Flora Lyndsay* represent love of home as a gender marker: 'Women ... feel parting with the old familiar places and faces, more keenly than men' ('Well in the Wilderness' 90). When Rachel Wilde first loses sight of home as a young child, she is reduced to tears: 'It was the hand of nature knocking at her unsophisticated heart, and demanding the sympathies, which had been planted and fostered, by the divine mother, unknown albeit, to her thoughtless offspring' ('Rachel Wilde' 105). While love of country is represented as common to both men and women, women are represented as emotionally attached to home and especially to siblings and parents in a way which is almost physically debilitating to a female emigrant.[6] The often remarked[7] reiteration of the narrator's homesickness in *Roughing It* might usefully be considered as part of the text's anxiety to establish its narrator's authority as a feminine woman. The importance of submission to authority, which is at once the authority of a husband and of God's Providence, is foregrounded by the narrator's feminine love of home and therefore her reluctance to emigrate. The narrator of *Roughing It* claims to have received a premonition warning her not to emigrate: 'how gladly I would have obeyed the injunction had it still been in my power. I had bowed to a superior mandate, the command of duty; for my husband's sake, for the sake of the infant, whose little bosom heaved against my swelling heart, I had consented to bid adieu for ever to my native shores' (194). The seeming contradiction posed by the assertion that love of home is part of feminine nature but that this nature must be denied in submitting to the natural authority of a husband is resolved by the attribution of self-control, endurance, and self-denial to the truly feminine woman.

The theme of submission to masculine authority is defined in *Flora Lyndsay* by the contrast created between Flora and two of her Scots acquaintances, Miss Carr and Mrs Ready. Mrs Ready's 'harsh, unfeminine voice and manners;[and] her assumption of learning and superiority, without any real title to either' (21) label her as insufficiently gendered. This judgment is confirmed by her vehement condemnation of marriage and her advice to Flora not to submit to her husband's decision to emigrate: 'I am none of your soft bread-and-butter wives, who consider it their *duty* to become the mere *echo* of their husbands. If *I* did not wish to go, no tyrannical lord of the creation, falsely so called, should compel me to act against my inclinations' (22). But Flora argues that if all marriages were unpleasant, and all men tyrannical, 'who would marry?' (23). For Flora (and by implication for the feminine woman), submission to masculine authority is redeemed by love, which effectively limits its exercise. Miss Carr condemns the submissive woman as characterless: 'These passive women are always great favorites with men. They have no decided character of their own, and become the mere echoes of superior minds' (44). However, Miss Carr's 'character' is decidedly masculine: she wears a man's hat, 'smoke[s] out of a long pipe, dr[inks] brandy-punch,' and 'swears like a man' (33–4). Her appearance is 'masculine and decidedly ugly' (34); 'even in youth' she was 'coarse and vulgar' (34), and it is apparent even to passing pedlars that she is not a lady (39). While her comments on manners and restrictive fashions in women's dress strike Flora as having 'a great deal of truth' (54), Flora is physically frightened of her wild behaviour and advises her to submit to the 'rules' (46) of feminine behaviour 'in order to avoid singularity' (42). In contrast, Flora displays her femininity by proving her utter inability to make simple decisions: when she defies her husband in order to take a walk in the mountains, she must be rescued after she is overcome by her fear of heights. By her actions, she disproves a gypsy prediction that she will 'wear the breeches' (146) in the family. 'If that was wearing the breeches,' she says, 'I am sure I disgraced them with my worse than womanish fears' (146).[8]

Roughing It in the Bush develops the opposition between feminine virtue and the career of writer, comparing the narrator's domestic failures and successes to her literary ambitions. In fact, the book explicitly denies her literary ambitions and argues that her self-esteem is dependent upon success in domestic life, which is represented as much more satisfying and important than resumption of her literary career. Commenting on the failure of her first attempt to bake bread, the narrator remarks, 'For myself, I could have borne the severest infliction from the pen of the most formidable critic with more fortitude than I bore the cutting up of my first loaf of bread' (*RI* 121), while Tom Wilson exclaims, 'Oh Mrs. Moodie! I hope you make better books than bread' (*RI* 121). Similarly, the narrator's success in finally milking the cow that terrifies her is more emotionally satisfying, she writes, than any literary success: 'Yes! I felt prouder of that milk than many an author of the best thing he ever wrote, whether in verse or prose' (*RI* 183). Actually living the life of helpmeet to her pioneer husband, she implies, resolves any hesitation in choosing between public career and private home.

In opposing feminine virtue and writing, Susanna Moodie was invoking an ideology of feminine nature which stressed modest silence as the feminine practice which confirmed the existence of a chaste inner self

(Poovey 3–47). The profession of writer was inconsistent with this ideal, not only because writing would necessarily distract from the dutiful performance of tasks assigned by husband and family, but because it seemed to foreground the personality and opinions of the author and express her desire for public notice. The metaphor of 'concealing her blue-stockings' is revealing in this context; the stockings suggesting, of course, the connection between female sexuality and female speech which Mary Poovey and others have suggested is constitutive of the nineteenth-century ideology of gender. Conformity to an ideal inner self characterized by modesty, chastity, and self-effacement made the writing of autobiography especially problematic for women writers, Sidonie Smith points out in *A Poetics of Women's Autobiography*. The normative definition of the genre rests on the autobiographer's claim to public notice, yet the truly feminine woman was supposed to have no such claim. The initial choice facing a woman autobiographer, Smith suggests, is whether to create herself according to the conventions of the genre, 'enacting the scenario of male selfhood' and 'thereby invit[ing] public censure' (8) for her unnatural conception, or to create herself as a conventionally feminine woman, whose life is rendered by definition a 'non-story' (50). 'However much she may desire to pursue the paternal narrative with its promise of power … she recognizes [that] … [h]er narrative may bring notoriety; and with notoriety can come isolation and the loss of love and acceptance in the culture that would hold her in its fictions' (54). The female autobiographer knows that her book will hold her up to judgment, not for her facility as a writer, but for her actions as a woman; in fact, many reviews of Susanna Moodie's work focused not on the literary elements of the text, but on the perceived relationship between the actions depicted in it and the moral value of the 'self' that motivated them (Ballstadt, Editor's Introduction xxx–xxxii).

Smith details the way that the nineteenth-century ideology of gender 'profoundly contaminated [women's] relationship to the pen as an instrument of power' (7) yet notes that women like Susanna Moodie continued to write; by conforming to the 'rules' of femininity (as Susanna Moodie called them), women were enabled to use the limited authority which those rules granted. Primary among these 'rules' is the requirement of selfless nurturance and care for husband and children, and *Roughing It in the Bush* mobilizes this ideal to authorize the narrator's desire to write. In fact, the feminine self of *Roughing It in the Bush* is represented as having no desire to write. She takes up her pen in 1838 solely to help her husband when all other means of earning money have been exhausted, and when honest people who have trusted John Dunbar Moodie to pay back their loans are on the verge of bankruptcy. She states that only 'the hope of being of the least service to those dear to [her]' (*RI* 417) leads her to resume her (supposedly) interrupted writing career in the bush. Only the prospect of contributing materially to the family welfare could justify her actions; as she says in the Introduction to *Mark Hurdlestone*, her 'time ... belonged by right to [her] family, and was too valuable a commodity to give away' (*Life* 286). Similarly, Flora Lyndsay distances herself from any positive desire to write when she offers apologetic explanations for her decision to write the tale of Noah Cotton. The activity will keep her from 'dwelling too much on the future' and so make her a better companion and more loving mother, Flora explains; the story itself might 'interest her husband' (215) and so justify her activity by serving the feminine function of 'animating [him] to fresh exertions' (95). The eventual publication of the tale of Noah Cotton by the modest Flora is suggested, as are all of her actions, by submission to her husband's wishes and his taste: 'Flora finished her story, but she wanted courage to read it to her husband, who was very fastidious about his wife's literary performances. And many years passed away ... before she again brought the time-worn manuscript to light, and submitted it to his critical eye. And because it pleased him, she ... thought that it might find favor with the public' (316). In *Roughing It* and *Life in the Clearings*, the narrator justifies her project in writing two autobiographical books by extending the domestic ideal of nurturance to her countrymen. *Roughing It*, she claims, fulfils her duty to warn prospective settlers of the lies and deceptions practised by unscrupulous land promoters and to protect the fair daughters of Albion from travails unsuited to their upbringing. Similarly, the introduction to *Life in the Clearings* modestly accounts for the appearance of the sequel to *Roughing It* by the numerous requests the narrator has received for an account of 'the present state of society in the colony' (xxxiii). Within both books, the speaker claims that her writing is a duty enjoined upon her by her desire to serve her husband, by the responsibility of raising her family, by obligations to her publisher, and, finally, by her own ill-health.

This retreat into the stereotype of feminine self-effacement allows the narrator to speak with the authority of the domestic woman. Moodie's narrator rejects the 'masculine' story and writes the 'feminine' non-story of her life; but rather than being silenced by the limits of femininity, the texts adopt strategies which conform to conventional feminine practice, and especially adopt self-effacement as a narrative stance. Happily, 'the self-effacing speaking posture ... conceals all faults, including the fault of ambition inherent in the presumption of writing her story at all' (Smith 54). These strategies create two of the most often remarked aspects of Moodie's autobiographical works: their generic instability and their loose structure. These aspects of her writing are not solely evidence of attempts to 'pad' the work for the publisher, to accommodate the Canadian experience, or to express supposed 'schizophrenic' attitudes to nature and culture; rather, they derive from the concept of a feminine inner self who paradoxically conforms to two prevailing stereotypes of feminine behaviour: the self-effacing domestic woman and the gossip. By appealing to the stereotype of self-effacement, Susanna Moodie frees herself into the loose structure of the private communication of women, a good gossip between two friends, a kind of subversive communication which empowers the domestic sphere and those in it as primary builders of the new society.

Critics of Susanna Moodie's work have found a fruitful area of inquiry in attempting to uncover a unified structure in *Roughing It in the Bush* or, at the very least, to determine what genre or genres the book may belong to. Most recent critics have recognized that the book, and Mrs Moodie's version of herself in it, is structured by elements of fictional genres,[9] yet they are unsettled by what Carol Shields calls the 'disturbing disconnectedness' and 'apparent lack of unity' (5) of Moodie's work. Many, including Shields and Helen Buss,[10] try to distinguish between a 'real' voice of an historical and intentional Mrs Moodie and the voices of various fictional discourses; they suggest that the passages which represent her personal struggles or offer detailed material description represent reality, while the romantic descriptions of nature and the formulaic declarations of patriotic fervour merely represent an inauthentic bowing to convention. A related approach suggests that *Roughing It* is intended to be a religious conversion narrative or a novel of individual growth and acceptance, and implies that whatever does not fit the model is an error in Moodie's execution. Susan Glickman argues that the book's inconsistencies mirror the inconsistencies and self-contradictions of 'human nature' (20), while, in a contrasting approach, John Thurston makes a virtue of the diversity of generic and historical voices in *Roughing It*, arguing that traditional genre could not have 'contain[ed] her Canadian material' (Thurston, 'Re-writing *Roughing It*' 199) because it represents the excess which is excluded by the concept of genre.

However, the criticism has not acknowledged that the narrator herself designates this structural instability as definitive of the feminine text in one of her numerous metafictional asides. She writes in *Life in the Clearings* that the capabilities of women writers are specific and limited, and that a grab-bag of amusing anecdotes, descriptions of life and of nature, and didactic opinions on moral questions is the limit of feminine capabilities.[11] Strong plot construction, implying the ability to create and follow logical and realistic sequences of events, is masculine territory. 'Women make good use of their eyes and ears, and paint scenes that amuse or strike their fancy with tolerable accuracy; but it requires the strong-thinking heart of man to anticipate events and trace certain results from particular causes. Women are out of their element when they attempt to speculate on these abstruse matters – are apt to incline too strongly to their own opinions – and jump at conclusions which are either false or unsatisfactory' (*Life* 207–8). The narrator mixes contradictory elements of autobiography, sentimental romance, conversion narrative, and how-to handbook with anecdote, natural description, and moral essay, confirming her feminine inability to plot, to 'trace certain results from particular causes.' The narrator simply functions, she says, as a faithful recorder of those incidents which appeal to her sense of fun and which seem illustrative of a 'life in the woods' (*RI* 305).[12]

The numerous tales within tales, anecdotes recounted by neighbours and friends, interpolated chapters, and poems by J.W.D. Moodie and by Samuel Strickland that characterize Susanna Moodie's autobiographical works suggest the truly feminine woman's self-effacement from the text which is her life. The heroine of *Flora Lyndsay*[13] is the author of an anonymous pamphlet in favour of the abolition of slavery and the tale 'Noah Cotton,' which is intended to amuse her husband, but both works are structured to divert attention away from the narrator, and to allow her to disclaim the creative responsibility of author. Flora explains that her abolitionist pamphlet was merely transcribed from the dictation of an escaped slave, and really gives her no claim to the name of author. The narrative of 'Noah Cotton,' an interpolated romance which takes up about one-third of the book, is a miracle of distancing techniques: Susanna Moodie writes a story of Flora Lyndsay; partway through this story, Flora writes a story of Noah Cotton; partway through this story, the voice of Flora disappears as Noah Cotton tells his own story; and partway through this story, Cotton's mother takes over to tell her own story in the first person. Thus Moodie's life is relegated to forming a frame narrative to the book *Flora Lyndsay*; the voice of the writer and her narrator, Flora, completely disappear from a work which is still seemingly autobiographical.

The pattern of self-effacement is repeated in *Roughing It* and *Life in the*

Clearings. Roughing It contains numerous dialogues from which the narrator disappears, such as the conversation between Tom Wilson and Betty Fye concerning the making of 'Bran emptyings' to use as a substitute for yeast. Tom Wilson narrates his own story, as does Malcolm, the 'stumpy man,' and Jenny, the faithful servant; neighbours narrate the story of Brian the Still-Hunter's past, anecdotes about Indian behaviour, and the story of Captain N—, Jenny's former master. J.W.D. Moodie narrates his own chapters (three in the first 1852 edition, and four in the second 1852 edition),[14] and Samuel Strickland, his partial chapter describing a whirlwind; in these cases, the narrator justifies her effacement from the text by claiming that as a woman she is not qualified to speak on the matters which concern men: 'I will leave my husband, who is better qualified than myself, to give a more accurate account of the country, while I turn to matters of a light and livelier cast' (*RI* 206). Similarly, in *Life in the Clearings*, chapters 5 and 6 are narrated by a travelling musician; anecdotes of religious 'camp meetings' are told by the voice of a 'friend' and by 'a beautiful young married lady'; the story of Grace Marks is told by her lawyer; that of Michael MacBride by three narrators; the story of Jeanie Burns's betrayal by her fiancé is told by James N—, a manservant; and the anecdotes of lost children are told by a Mrs H—, the wife of a man who farms for the Moodies on shares.

The narrator's continual denials of her authority to speak on almost any issue have been remarked by many readers, especially as the books themselves seem to contradict these protestations. The narrator's denial that she is qualified to speak conclusively about Canada may have been an attempt to defend herself against charges levelled by Canadians that Susanna Moodie misrepresents Canada; and an entire section of *Life in the Clearings* is devoted to refuting such charges arising from the publication of *Roughing It.* Yet numerous asides in *Roughing It* and *Life in the Clearings* refer to a gendered division of literary texts in which only the masculine author may claim authority over certain subjects and literary structures. 'As a woman, I cannot enter into the philosophy of these things, nor is it my intention to do so. I leave statistics for wiser and cleverer male heads' (*Life* 38). The narrator's denials of her authority to speak on matters of political or economic interest, her appeal to the stereotype of feminine intellectual superficiality, seem to have the effect of freeing her into the realm of domestic authority. She goes on to specify and develop many subjects of interest and importance to the 'intending emigrant' – many of which, by her own definition, belong exclusively to the realm of masculine commentary. The class system, the relative merits of monarchy and republicanism, insanity, overpopulation, the lack of firewood in established Canadian communities, the strife between adherents of the Catholic and Protestant religions, political upheavals in the colony, the reasons behind the rebellion of 1837, and the prospects for the Reform cause are all topics of the narrator's commentary in *Life in the Clearings* and *Roughing It.*

Self-effacement gives way to another stereotype, that of the woman's wagging tongue, to give these texts the domestic voice of gossip. Susanna Moodie's books convey information in the form of anecdote, moral judgment, and domestic detail – the intimate information of the domestic sphere which convention grants to women. *Life in the Clearings* specifically invokes the model of gossip in the first chapter, when the narrator figuratively invites the reader: 'Come take your seat with me on the deck of the steamer; and as we glide over the waters of this beautiful Bay of Quinte, I will make you acquainted with every spot worthy of note along its picturesque shores' (4). She apologetically invokes the stereotype of woman as gossip to excuse the shapelessness and diversity of her conversation: 'Allow me a woman's privilege of talking of all sorts of things by the way. Should I tire you with my desultory mode of conversation, bear with me charitably, and take into account the infirmities incidental to my gossiping sex' (*Life* 4). Her description of the situation in which her book will be read also suggests the intimacy of gossip; her book is 'a small volume which may help to while away an idle hour, or fill up the blanks of a wet day' (xxxiii), as conversation with a trusted friend would do. Like gossip, the books show interest in surface details of domestic and social life, and are composed of 'stories' which are complete in themselves, containing fabula, characters, and moral commentary (Spacks, *Gossip* 15).

Both *Roughing It* and *Life* proceed like a conversation: a topic is introduced, a moral judgment passed upon it, and many examples given to illustrate the rightness of that judgment. The narrator of *Roughing It* recounts stories about her neighbours, Old Satan, Uncle Joe, and Brian the Still-Hunter; about borrowing, Indians, bees, and charivaris. The narrator of *Life* tells us anecdotes about religious conversions, about dances and social gatherings, about alcoholism in the colony, about wearing mourning, and about multitudes of other topics. Yet the examples are not simply examples, but stories in their own right, with beginnings, middles, and ends. The moral judgments rely upon the intimacy of shared values, an aspect of gossip Spacks identifies as crucial (84); the narrator addresses persons of her own class, religious views, and background, domestic women who might be similarly expected to deplore the custom of wearing mourning for its hypocrisy and its waste of money, to con-

demn the system of 'borrowing' when practised along Yankee lines, and
to applaud her eventual reconciliation to God and the will of her husband in entering into the project of emigration wholeheartedly.

The idea of evil gossip has always been associated with women, according to Spacks, ever since 'Eve, a woman, brought sin into the world by
unwise speaking and unwise listening' (41). Susanna Moodie acknowledges the patriarchal stereotype of the uncontrolled and uncontrollable
woman's tongue in her comments on the Puritan name 'Silence Shar-
man' in *Roughing It*: 'Was the woman deaf and dumb, or did her friends
hope by bestowing upon her such an impossible name to still the voice of
Nature, and check, by an admonitory appellative, the active spirit that
lives in the tongue of woman?' (*RI* 127). Yet the 'active spirit' who learns
about her world through revelation of intimate detail in a conversational
setting is the focus of both *Roughing It* and *Life*. Bina Freiwald notes in an
article on *Roughing It*, 'If we stilled or silenced the "voice of nature" which
[the narrator] finds distilled in the "active spirit that lives in the tongue of
woman" little would remain of the life of the story' (160); perhaps, to go
further, nothing would be left of the story. In direct opposition to her
concurrent denials of the importance of her writing, the narrator claims
that the elements of gossip in her work are more important, and more
communicative, than any formal structure could be, to those who have
the wit to understand: 'The real character of a people can be more truly
gathered from such seemingly trifling incidents than from any ideas we
may form of them from the great facts in their history and this is my reason for detailing events which might otherwise appear insignificant and
unimportant' (*RI* 290). The importance of domestic gossip as an alternative to public forms of communication is illustrated in the 'Walk to Dum-
mer' section of *Roughing It*, for the narrator learns about the starving wife
of the delinquent Captain N— by way of gossip related by servants and by
her friend Emilia S—. Her journey to ascertain the truth of such gossip
and to bring relief to the starving family is proof of the efficacy of gossip
in circumventing the humiliation and social censure which a public
appeal for help would have created.

Susanna Moodie's conformity to the stereotype of feminine self-effacement is the strategy that allows her to write herself into the text; it frees
her into the realm of domestic authority, and allows her to communicate
effectively the information on the social life and economic conditions of
Canada, which are the real necessities for an emigrant. As the narrator
says: 'if this book is regarded not as a work of amusement but one of practical experience ... it will not fail to convey some useful hints to those who

have contemplated emigration to Canada' (*RI* 444). Her justification of writing as a feminine practice effectively hides the 'objectionable colour' of her blue-stockings and shows the face of the 'tamest commonplace' to her readers. The structure of non-structure, of gossip and personal anecdote, also implies the importance of the details of day-to-day domestic and social life in determining the success of the project of emigration and the nature of the new country, and so empowers the domestic sphere and those confined to it.

3

Translated by Desire: Romance and Politics in Rosanna Leprohon's Antoinette de Mirecourt

Slave and sovereign at once, she was willing to obey because it was in her power to reign.

Honoré de Balzac, *A Woman of Thirty*

Part way through *Antoinette de Mirecourt*, Colonel Evelyn recounts an anecdote in which King George III compliments a French-Canadian matron: the King reportedly told the lady that 'if all the Canadian ladies resemble[d] her, he had indeed good reason to feel proud of his fair conquest' (167). In this anecdote, the meaning of the word 'conquest' is ambiguous: while it refers conventionally to the military conquest of Quebec by the British forces and its concession by France as part of the Treaty of Paris in 1763, its modification by the adjective 'fair,' drawn from the vocabulary of courtly love poetry to designate a desirable love object, allows 'conquest' to refer to securing affections as well as authority. While Evelyn's auditors remark that the Canadian delegation at King George's court 'ha[s] been sent to represent our interests, as well as to present the expression of our homage to our new monarch,' further discussion of the King's compliment reinterprets the delegation's political aims within the conventions of romance; Sternfield quips, 'And behold it is His Majesty who pays homage instead' (167).

This anecdote, and Sternfield's 'gallant' reinterpretation of it, offers a pattern for the way that *Antoinette de Mirecourt* uses the concept of feminine domestic authority to rewrite political relationships of military dominance and forced subordination in post-Conquest Quebec as relations of equality and choice by translating them into gender relations. In *Antoinette*, the conquest of Quebec by British forces and its subsequent rule by 'those who are aliens alike to our race, creed, and tongue' (*Antoinette* 83) is domesticated by its representation as an extended courtship and con-tained within the romantic teleology which prescribes ideological closure in heterosexual marriage. But by interpreting marriage within the con-ventions of the 'sexual contract,' *Antoinette* represents that relationship, not as one of submission to imperial power, but as a partnership freely chosen by equal participants, based upon desirable individual characteris-tics rather than upon cultural affiliation or nationalistic political aims. While Quebec may be forced to pay political homage to King George, according to the conventions of romance, George in turn pays homage to *les belles Québécoises.* This approach empowers femininity within the econ-omy of heterosexual exchange, creating all issues of political tension as problems of individual moral behaviour and thus under the authority of feminine power to restrain and guide. The novel conceals a critique of British imperial power within a debate about marriage, empowering women in general and Leprohon in particular to make interpretive state-ments about Quebec history and to pass judgment upon the behaviour of the British crown towards Quebec.

In the latter part of the nineteenth century, historical romances like *Antoinette de Mirecourt* were one of the culturally approved media for such an argument. Despite a lingering cultural bias against fiction as a whole, historical fiction was generally approved in English Canada as the appro-priate genre for mass audiences: following the model of Walter Scott, his-torical fiction was supposed to offer the heroes and heroines of the past as suitable models for principled behaviour in the present, and to foster a sense of 'nationhood' in the creation of a shared social mythology.[1] John Richardson's *Wacousta* (1832) and its sequel, *The Canadian Brothers* (1840), drew upon the 'Indian wars' of the 1760s and the War of 1812, respectively, to articulate relationships between English and French Canadians, the United States, and First Nations people at the founding of Upper Canada. Quebec held a privileged place as a setting for Gothic and romantic historical fiction early in the century, as English-Canadian writ-ers projected onto French Canada their desire for cultural distinctiveness as well as their cultural biases against Catholicism and supposed peasant 'backwardness.' As the century progressed, Quebec became a mine of 'material' for local colourists and folk-realist writers as these genres became popular.[2]

Novels like *Antoinette de Mirecourt* and William Kirby's *The Golden Dog* (1877) articulate a generalized cultural anxiety around the time of Con-federation to create a narrative of English-Canadian nationhood which justified the inclusion of Quebec. William Kirby's book is by far the best known of the two, and it represents what would become the dominant

English-Canadian narrative of the fall of Quebec. *The Golden Dog* was inspired by a book of sketches from Quebec history by John Lemoine, *Maple Leaves* (1863), and derived its historical information from *Pioneers of France in the New World* (1863), by American Francis Parkman. From Lemoine, the book takes episodes of Gothic horror, including the story of the poisoner and witch, La Corriveau; but Parkman determines the portrayal of the fall of Quebec as the welcome liberation of the Québécois from domination by a corrupt French court into the freedoms of British subjects. Parkman argued that by 1760 honest Québécois peasants and bourgeois were suffering under the yoke of exploitation by greedy and unscrupulous representatives of the French crown; *The Golden Dog* follows Parkman in representing the upper classes of Quebec as abandoning their responsibilities when the British approached, suggesting that the subsequent British dominance of Quebec by a military government was justified because only uneducated 'habitants' remained in the colony. *Antoinette de Mirecourt* opposes this dominant narrative[3] from an ambivalent position between the French- and English-Canadian communities. In contrast to *The Golden Dog*, *Antoinette* draws its historical information from a French-Canadian authority, François-Xavier Garneau, and is at pains to show not only that the educated classes in Quebec behaved responsibly towards their countrymen, but that they remained in the colony after the Conquest. *Antoinette* avoids the sensational stereotypes of Catholicism – scheming Jesuits, self-interested priests, and young girls 'buried alive' in convents – that characterized many English-Canadian stories of Quebec life. *Antoinette* also creates situations which illustrate the legitimate grievances of the Québécois against British military government. However, the novel makes these points by avoiding the public world of Intendant Bigot and the Bourgeois Philibert and focusing on the domestic world of the salon and the boudoir. Like other English-Canadian novels of the Conquest, *Antoinette* finally justifies British rule of Quebec, though it does so in accordance with the decorum of gender and genre by translating issues of political dominance and submission into gender issues, and resolving them according to the 'sexual contract.'

Although romances like *Antoinette* and *The Golden Dog* dominated the literary scene in Canada in the nineteenth and early twentieth centuries,[4] they are generally dismissed by contemporary Canadian critics as examples of an inferior literary form not worthy of sustained critical attention. Postcolonial and feminist critics, like the early realist novelists, treat 'romantic' views of women's role as part and parcel of their oppression, and celebrate their replacement with more 'realistic' representations of women's role.[5] Criticism of *Antoinette de Mirecourt* follows this pattern. John Stockdale, in the *Dictionary of Canadian Biography* entry on Rosanna Leprohon, initially judges *Antoinette* to be 'the worst of' Leprohon's Canadian novels (*DCB* 10:537)[6] because it is her most 'romantic'; he modified this evaluation in his introduction to the CEECT edition of the novel, not because he has changed his opinion of romance, but because he now believes *Antoinette* to be realistic (xiii).[7] In addition, Stockdale's analysis (and that of John Sorfleet in his introduction to *The Manor House of de Villerai*) suggests a major criticism of Leprohon's work is its seeming disconnection from 'the political world run by men' (Armstrong 4). Indeed, those critics who have argued that *Antoinette* represents an important commentary upon 'French-English relations in Canada' (Edwards, 'Essentially Canadian' 9) have done so by bracketing off the actual love story. Klinck, Edwards, Stockdale, and MacMillan, McMullen, and Waterston discuss setting as well as short passages of social satire or realistic description, and offer the attitudes of various characters towards imperial power as examples of historical political positions.[8] The romance itself is deemed to be the spoonful of sugar which hides the medicine, thus 'essentially' trivial and certainly dispensable.

In viewing the romance as primarily 'amusement for women readers of early Canada' (Stockdale, *DCB* 10:538), the critics repeat the gesture that the romance itself enacts: the separation of the personal and the political, and the production of gender as a primary category of self-definition. Works like *Desire and Domestic Fiction* (Armstrong) and *Sensational Designs* (Tompkins) have shown how the popular romance in Britain and the United States participated in the gendering of discourse, producing the 'domestic sphere' of courtship, marriage, and moral and emotional life by limiting the definition of the political and radically excluding it from home and family. Novels set in colonial New France or eighteenth- and nineteenth-century Nova Scotia may teem with historical detail, or even historical characters, but the public realm of politics is limited to men, and the 'love stories' of LeGardeur or Intendant Bigot are confined strictly to the feminine boudoir, where the moral influence of the truly feminine woman becomes a powerful force.

According to the 'sexual contract,' men protect women in return for their domestication; 'the female relinquishes political control to the male in order to acquire exclusive authority over domestic life, emotions, taste, and morality' (Armstrong 41). The fiction of the 'sexual contract' ensures that individuals are distinguished, first and foremost, by gender: gendered individuals must pre-exist the contract in order to 'desire' their 'self-perfection' through heterosexual marriage. Secondly, the 'sexual contract' requires that gendered individuals seem to exercise free choice in entering into heterosexual marriage, and so presupposes a process of selection whereby individuals determine their own marriage partners irrespective of cultural affiliation. The basis of that choice must be gender; the inner self of the potential partner is produced in order to discover its correspondence to the surface appearance of natural gender. Finally, the 'sexual contract' universalizes and heterosexualizes desire, by making the practice of gender (the ability to embody a gender ideal) the most important aspect of a potential marriage partner, rather than kinship affiliation or sexual desirability. Thus the 'sexual contract' offers a narrative pattern whereby individuals come to an understanding of themselves and their potential partners in relation to a narrowly prescribed gender ideal which purports to equalize their power in relation to each other; the man utilizes his power to protect and shelter the woman, and she exercises her power over him through her influence over his heart. This paradigm, common throughout the history of the novel,[9] succeeded earlier narrative forms in which the desirability of marriage partners varied according to birth, wealth, class, and culture.

Thus *Antoinette* and other nineteenth-century romances are radically political in that they presume to define and confine discourse according to naturalized genders; they confer authority upon both male and female speakers according to their gender, and so provide a position from which feminine authority can be asserted. These are not trivial issues, but formative in the developing discourse of nationhood in which both writers and critics engaged in nineteenth- and early twentieth-century Canada. These works claim the authority of the feminine sphere to rewrite public and political issues as gender issues, and therefore to subject them to the moral judgment associated with the feminine realm. Such works subordinate aesthetic issues such as unity and character development to the generic requirements which reader and writer held in common – the desire to impose an interpretive pattern upon political issues: 'by thus subordinating all social differences to those based on gender ... these novels bring order to social relationships' (Armstrong 4).

In *Desire and Domestic Fiction*, Nancy Armstrong argues that by the nineteenth century 'it had been established that novels were supposed to rewrite political history as personal histories that elaborated on the courtship procedures ensuring a happy domestic life' (38). She recounts the way that the British romance domesticated conflict between the aristocratic and middle classes by promoting an ideal of gender which existed apart from class or kinship affiliations. Leprohon's novel *Armand Durand; or, A Promise Fulfilled* (1868) conforms to this initial pattern by domesticating class issues in Quebec as an extended discussion of courtship and marriage in the New World. In *Armand Durand* four wives with diverse class backgrounds are represented, and their various abilities to represent the gender ideal effectively detach gender from class, defining femininity as the practice of control and self-control which derives from a completely gendered inner self. Armand's father, Paul, a prosperous farmer, proposes marriage to Geneviève, a well-born but poverty-stricken French nursery maid visiting the local seigneur. He chooses her because her helpless femininity confirms his masculine protectiveness: 'She was so delicate, so helpless-looking in appearance, so desolate, so unhappy in reality, that he could not avoid feeling that species of inward impulse which all noble, manly men know in the presence of oppressed weakness, the desire to protect and succor [*sic*]' (4). Geneviève is a hopeless housekeeper and utterly incapable of adding anything other than gracefulness and love to her husband's comfort; yet she gains control over him in marrying him and is able, simply through the gentleness 'naturally' a part of her gender, to overpower his jealousy: 'that feminine gentleness, more powerful than anger, logic or pride, had demolished in an instant the wall that passion and suspicion had raised between them' (15). Paul Durand's second wife is unable to create the atmosphere of loving connection to her husband because he is still grieving over Geneviève, yet her skill as a housekeeper, her love for the orphaned Armand, and her eventual production of a second son endear her to her husband.

Armand grows up to exemplify the elegant upper-class graces of his French mother; yet he chooses to marry Delima, a lower-class *canadienne* whose actions suggest she is modest, shy, and gentle. Yet Delima's appearance masks a true self insufficiently gendered, and after her marriage she becomes a shrew who demands her husband furnish clothes and servants to suit her social ambitions. Delima is convinced that her accession to the class of 'gentlefolk' will be secured by her exhibition of an aggressive air of superiority, and thus 'endeavoured to make up by arrogance and constant fault-finding for the want of that calm justice and perfect self command so necessary to those whose lot it is to govern' (61). While Delima resembles Armand's mother in being an inefficient housekeeper, unlike Geneviève she lacks the femininity which would allow her 'to render his home so happy' (55) as to make such material deficiencies meaningless. Armand's true mate and the novel's real comparison to Geneviève is the unconventionally aristocratic Gertrude, identifiable by her ability to com-

mand the true feminine power of her moral authority. When Armand is
in despair over his relationship with his wife, and in danger of leaving his
profession and becoming a drunkard, Gertrude exacts a promise from
him, 'by the memory of the parents who so dearly loved [him]' (69), to
become an abstainer. After Delima's death in childbirth, Armand marries
Gertrude and surrenders his moral choices to her guardianship: 'How
can I say no to any request of yours?' (76), he exclaims after the marriage.

Armand Durand suggests that the suitable wife for a rising son of peasant Québécois parents must be able to assist her husband to the extent of
controlling her own selfish desires and putting his welfare, and that of his
career, first. While Geneviève is well born, she has experienced poverty
and humiliation as a servant in the home of a relative; she is grateful to
have been rescued, and that gratitude, expressed as gentle submission
and undemanding love, is a mark of gender rather than class. Delima's
social ambition is interpreted by the text as her 'unwomanly harshness,
her weak fretful waywardness' (70), in other words, as a lack of naturalized femininity. While Gertrude is of aristocratic birth, she is also dependent upon the charity of her rich uncle; Gertrude's moral authority
finally derives from her authority as a woman, not her social class. Conformity to a gender ideal of self-sacrifice and moral virtue overwrites class
and cultural affiliation, erasing the social boundaries between the rural
peasant class and the urban descendants of seigneurs and remaking
social divisions according to gender alone.

In *Antoinette de Mirecourt* a similar development is mapped, as class and
cultural affiliation are overridden by the characteristics of naturalized
gender as the basis for a successful marriage alliance. Antoinette's father
holds the view that the choice of a marriage partner must be based upon
class and cultural affiliation, and accordingly he is adamantly opposed to
contracting any sort of alliance with the English through a marriage
between his daughter and an Englishman, no matter how noble and
'manly.' He 'hates the very name' (10) of the English, and further
instructs Antoinette to 'watch well over her affections, and bestow them
on none of the gay strangers who might visit her cousin's house, for assur-
edly he would never under any circumstances countenance any of them
as her suitors' (35). De Mirecourt's antipathy to the English is based upon
his experience of the 'oppressive acts of the new government' (121) and
his understanding that a marriage between Antoinette and a British
officer would constitute a political alliance with the oppressors; when
Lucille D'Aulnay suggests that Antoinette may meet 'with some noble,
good man, who apart from the objection of his being a foreigner ... [is]

himself worthy in all other things of her affection –' (73–4) de Mirecourt is adamant that no such personal characteristics would change his determination. His choice for Antoinette's future husband is, accordingly, Louis Beauchesne, her close friend from childhood and 'an excellent *parti* too in a worldly point of view' (82), though Antoinette objects: 'I do not love him sufficiently well to marry him' (81).

The novel offers qualified arguments for the success of such an arranged marriage. The marriage of Lucille and Mr D'Aulnay, arranged by Lucille's parents and in the face of her opposition, has been happy and long-lasting, despite Mrs D'Aulnay's opinion that 'the only sure basis for a happy marriage, is mutual love, and community of soul and feeling' (12). However, a completely arranged marriage is offered as arbitrary and old-fashioned in a society that purports to respect feeling over material possessions. Lucille argues, 'What right has [your father] to dispose of you ... as if you were a farm or field he wished to get rid of?' (73).

A stronger testimony in favour of a marriage with Louis is offered by the parallel marriage of Antoinette's parents, who, like Antoinette and Louis, had been intimate since childhood. Antoinette's mother, Corinne, an orphan raised in the de Mirecourt household, is gendered by the 'maiden pride and modesty' which leads her to conceal 'the devoted love that had grown with the young girl's growth, and become an engrossing sentiment of her life' (18). De Mirecourt, performing his protective role with a 'delicate sense of honour [and] chivalrous generosity of character' (20), feels bound by the self-sacrificing and loyal nature of her love to marry her, and is rewarded by the growth of an answering affection which is lifelong.

The marriage of Antoinette's parents, while not 'arranged' in the strict sense, offers a clear pattern of criteria which should guide the choice of a desirable marriage partner in the absence of parental authority. Corinne's modestly hidden inner self confirms her conformity to a gender ideal which values a sense of familial duty, emotional warmth, self-sacrifice, and self-command. The production of these 'depths' within the character of Corinne makes the marriage possible. De Mirecourt is initially repulsed by the 'fair exterior' of Corinne because he believes 'so little feeling or warmth of character lurked beneath' (17). His discovery of her love for him, concealed in deference to his happiness and that of his mother, creates her as a complex subject with a fully feminine interior life as well as a beautiful and female exterior. For the interior qualities produced by the narrative, or, as the text would have it, unwittingly 'revealed,' de Mirecourt considers her a desirable wife.

Upon these criteria, Louis Beauchesne is an eminently desirable husband. He not only appears to perform the role of masculine protector,
but he is able to dissemble the warmth of his affections in order to save
Antoinette the heartache of denying her old friend; he commands his
feelings because, as he says, 'I seek Antoinette's happiness before my
own' (85). However, his conformity to his gender role is also what makes
his marriage to Antoinette impossible. As a young Canadian man proud
of his race and heritage, Louis daily risks clashes with the English. While
Antoinette's 'quizzing' of the English fop Sir Percy DeLaval is taken as a
joke by his fellow officers, Louis's parallel mocking of Sternfield is a
deadly insult. Older men like D'Aulnay can avoid the English in their
libraries, but Louis's gendered role as protector of his home (which is
both Quebec and Antoinette's honour) dictates his inevitable involve-
ment in a duel; a 'real' man, in such circumstances, must fight. However,
as representative of masculine Quebec, Louis has already failed in his role
as protector, for the British have won; his flight from the country is thus
inevitable.

Notably, the nationalist political arguments often advanced in Québécois fiction for confining the choice of a marriage partner to Catholic
Québécois are absent. The convenient 'voices of Quebec' who descend
to advise Maria Chapdelaine to consider *la race* above all do not advise
Antoinette to choose Louis, nor do the other characters consider the
marriage in this light. The novel makes the case in Louis's favour on the
basis of his gender, his role as protector of Quebec and of Antoinette,
expressed as his capacity for deep feeling and self-sacrifice in the performance of this role, though de Mirecourt's approval is an additional fac-
tor.[10] It also disqualifies Louis from the marriage on the basis of his
gender; he has failed to protect Antoinette/Quebec and is no longer in a
position to do so, and thus Antoinette must seek another protector.

The British officer Audley Sternfield initially appears in this role, offering Antoinette an alternative to a forced marriage with Louis. However,
his refusal to moderate his ardour in the face of her evident discomfort
sounds a warning bell; such behaviour is not 'manly,' in that it takes
advantage of her weakness. The secret marriage confirms this warning,
for by insisting upon it Sternfield asks Antoinette to transgress the 'sacred
rules of feminine delicacy, the holy dictates of filial duty' (158) and thus
to betray her own gender. His subsequent refusal to submit to Antoinette's feminine authority in moderating his behaviour signals that Antoinette's first marriage does not conform to the 'sexual contract'; while
it requires that she surrender herself to her husband, it confers no corre-

sponding hold upon his heart and hence no moral authority over his behaviour. The failure of the marriage to confer equality upon the partners according to the 'sexual contract' is emphasized by the additional 'vows' which the two parties contract. Antoinette insists that Audley 'consent to waive, for the present, a husband's authority and privileges' (93) until their marriage has been made public, and solemnized by a Catholic ceremony in conformity with her piety and her duty; however, in return, he forces her to keep the marriage secret, an act designed to protect himself, not her.

The failure of Antoinette's first marriage is predicated on her own momentary lapse from the strictures of gender; she later regrets the 'senseless ill-judged passion which led' (158) her to consent to a secret Protestant marriage. 'She had violated the dictates of conscience and religion – trampled on a daughter's most sacred duties' (212) in defying her father, and she recognizes her sin in her inability to pray after the ceremony. While the novel places some of the blame upon Antoinette's advisers, particularly Lucille, and upon a somewhat indulgent upbringing by her father, Antoinette takes all the blame upon herself as she recognizes that when she consented to the marriage, 'passion at that moment spoke louder in her heart than principle' (70). However, despite the lapse which her marriage to Sternfield represents, Antoinette is coded by the text as essentially feminine. 'Antoinette's nature was loving and gentle,' and 'the passing fancy which she had mistaken for love, would ultimately have ripened into deep affection' had her husband 'proved persistently gentle and considerate' (109). She exemplifies 'self-command' (47) when she is thrown from the sleigh at the Lachine Rapids; her love of children and simple domesticity give her 'a charm which her beauty had never, perhaps, possessed in saloon or ball-room'(45). She prefers nature and natural scenery to artificial conversation (41) and shows pity for animals. Her silence conveys the modesty which forbids any attempt to 'profit' by her chance meetings with Evelyn.

More importantly, Antoinette is utterly unable to hide her emotions; the validity of her gendered inner self is written upon her body with the specificity of language, and her blushes and 'look[s] of intense mental pain' (99) reveal her duplicitous relationship to Sternfield in spite of her vow. This inability to dissemble her feelings is emphasized by contrast with Lucille, who advises Antoinette to regulate her feelings in order to achieve a deceptive surface impression: 'never allow anxiety or grief to go farther than imparting a delicate pallor or pensive look to your features' (112). However, Antoinette's inner anguish forces her body to display its authenticity as she declines into illness. When Sternfield injures Antoinette by pressing her wedding band into her flesh, Antoinette welcomes the injury, which externalizes and makes visible the pain which her marriage has inflicted: 'Why should not the outward symbol of our ill-starred union torture and crush the body as deeply as its reality does the soul?' (148).

The secrecy of her marriage creates a disjunction between Antoinette's actions and inner self – her practice and her essence – which alienates Colonel Evelyn's love for her. Isolated in an inner room during a ball at Lucille's, Antoinette submits to Sternfield's caress before the gaze of Evelyn, who responds by condemning Antoinette as a 'finished, faultless actress' (176). Her denials of love for Sternfield suggest to him that her feminine appearance conceals an unwomanly immodesty. Yet her 'guileless young nature' (99) is utterly incapable of dissembling, and later, when Evelyn learns of the secret marriage, he acknowledges, 'I read in your face that you spoke truth'(197). Finally, Antoinette is able to restore the correspondence between appearance and reality in her marriage when she hurries to Sternfield's deathbed: ''Tis my duty' (215), she says, emphasizing that in appearing to transgress the rules of feminine modesty, she is but reasserting her conformity to the domestic ideal.

Sternfield's surface appearance conceals rather than reveals his deviation from the code of masculinity. 'Trained in deceit' (174) by the fashionable life he has led, Sternfield's attractively masculine surface masks his inability to govern his own emotions and desires in the service of a 'manly' protectiveness towards women. Sternfield most thoroughly transgresses his gender role when he proves to be a 'tyrant' rather than a protector. His mercenary motive for marrying Antoinette is made clear when she is threatened with disinheritance; far from protecting her, he intends to exploit her. Antoinette accuses him: 'Profaning the sacred name of husband, you have been to me only a cruel, heartless tyrant. Prevented by sordid paltry motives of interest from acknowledging our marriage, you would yet wish to degrade me in my own eyes, in those of others' (171).

The use of the word 'tyrant' to describe Sternfield represents a fissure in the radical exclusions which constitute gender in the novel. The realms of politics and romance, defined as separate according to the 'sexual contract,' which relegates men to the former and women to the latter (and which are literally separated in the novel by the confinement of the 'historical background' to a separate chapter),[11] seem to overlap when the British Sternfield appears in the French-Canadian drawing-room in his political character as representative of the martial government, characterized in chapter 5 as 'that most insupportable of all tyrannies' (28).

The translation of the political into the domestic breaks down and provides a glimpse of the argument which the book conceals; if, like those of Antoinette and Sternfield, the 'destinies' of Canada and Great Britain have been 'irrevocably united' (28), then Canada, no less than Antoinette, possesses the moral authority to restrain and guide the actions of her imperial 'protector.'

Antoinette's authority is restored when she returns to feminine behaviour by confessing her sin to God, and vowing to avoid Sternfield until he is prepared to acknowledge her openly as his wife and allow a Catholic religious ceremony. Her calm resolve shocks Sternfield, and affects him: 'At times when her rare beauty, her wondrous grace, rises mentally before me, I feel she is a creature to be madly worshipped; then again, when she stands forth opposed to me, with that relentless firmness, that iron will, so strangely at variance with her usual character, her feminine loveliness ... I certainly love her more now than when I wooed and won her' (188–9). Her attitude to her marital obligations consists in the 'self-sacrificing heroism' (153) by which she considers herself bound to her husband despite his behaviour. The novel emphasizes that the element of free choice which governed Antoinette's marriage binds her more securely to the gender ideal of the dutiful wife who must endure her husband's mistreatment: because her marriage is a 'chain [she] ... forged for [her]self,' she 'must wear it to the end' (158). Her return to this feminine ideal allows the powerful assertion of her authority in the sphere of Sternfield's moral behaviour. She almost succeeds in controlling him, as he admits to himself when he withdraws to allow her to visit her father in peace: 'she is a mere child yet, and still how thoroughly, how completely she keeps me in check' (188). The final confirmation of her femininity occurs at Sternfield's deathbed, where he asks for her forgiveness: 'Your patient gentleness has touched me at last, and before I go hence, I would ask you to pardon me for all that I have made you suffer, for all my past cruelty and injustice' (231).

The source of feminine power in the novel is the 'heart,' and the discourse of the heart differentiates Evelyn and Sternfield. Evelyn reveals the 'depths' of his inner self when he recounts to Antoinette his story of betrayal, 'stooping to lay bare his proud heart to her gaze' (137). This inner self is designated by Antoinette's repeated reference to him as a 'true-hearted man,' in contrast to Sternfield, whose utter superficiality is signalled by his designation, 'heartless' (143). Evelyn's heart, like Antoinette's, is covered over, hidden; yet each is revealed by involuntary looks and expressions: 'what volumes of meaning, of emotion, were in that glance!' (145). While both hide an inner truth, they do so from motives of modesty, pain, and self-sacrifice; their innocence is writ large upon their faces, despite their ability to conceal it from the casual eye.

Because Evelyn is a 'true-hearted man,' he is susceptible to Antoinette's moral guidance; he loves her because her modesty and sincerity restore his faith in the 'sexual contract.' Colonel Evelyn was deceived in his first engagement with a beautiful 'girl of good family and gentle bringing up' (132) whose inner self so far deviated from the standard of femininity that she eloped from the altar with his richer, titled brother. As he explains to Antoinette, bitterness over this affair has blighted his life and is the source of his reputation as a misanthrope, for he has 'lost faith in' (134) women as a sex. Yet when Antoinette begs him not to challenge Sternfield to a duel, Evelyn agrees, and 'he inwardly rejoiced that his heart was not yet so utterly insensible as to be able to resist [her] influence' (141). And when he proposes marriage to her for the second and last time, he calls upon her to 'guide [him] back' to 'merciful God' through her 'counsels and examples' (235).

Antoinette's emergence from her 'brain fever' into a second marriage with Colonel Evelyn secures her moral authority over him. Her first marriage has taught her the evils of deviating from feminine behaviour; in addition, her mistakes have matured her and made her less naïve. She has become a fit partner for the world-weary and experienced Evelyn, who is ten years older and a former prisoner in the Napoleonic wars. Her ordeal has both proved her femininity and equalized their relationship, as Evelyn exclaims to her: 'as gold out of the furnace, so have you come purified and perfected out of your fiery trial – all that I had first thought, first hoped you were' (235).

De Mirecourt approves the marriage, for he has already met and come to admire Evelyn during the course of his trip to Quebec City. While he laments over what he finds there ('all ruins and ashes' [160]), he rejoices in having met our hero, who shows himself to be a 'person of high intellect, but also a just and liberal man' (161). In addition, when de Mirecourt recounts his meeting with Evelyn, it becomes clear that Evelyn has not revealed his thwarted and passionate attachment to Antoinette; his self-command and self-sacrifice, in order to protect the old man from embarrassment, are evident. De Mirecourt revises his blanket condemnation of Englishmen based upon the 'manly courtesy ... honour' (161), unselfishness, and hard work displayed by Evelyn, and he tells Antoinette: 'I could have forgiven you if you had succeeded in winning this gallant Englishman's homage' (163). De Mirecourt's old-fashioned reliance upon cultural affiliation in the choice of a marriage partner is rejected in favour of a choice based upon gender.

One incident recounted by de Mirecourt, however, represents another of the fissures in the text which allow the discourse of politics to invade the romance. De Mirecourt has witnessed Evelyn's defence of a *habitant* farmer who was victimized by 'one of the newly-arrived colonists who have come to lord it over ourselves and fallen fortunes' (162). Evelyn's actions prove his 'horror of anything like oppression'(161) in relations between British and Canadians, and de Mirecourt judges him to be 'totally free from the prejudices that rule so many of his caste and race' (160). Here Evelyn is singled out from the British imperial forces as a manly protector of the oppressed; the political issue of the structural relations which allow the British to oppress the French is resolved in the discovery of a 'true-hearted man.' However, de Mirecourt unwittingly reveals the reason why Evelyn has been so solicitous: he exclaims that Evelyn 'showed as much wish to assist and relieve me as if I had some lawful claim upon him' (164). The 'lawful claim,' of course, is Evelyn's desire to marry Antoinette and to thereby become de Mirecourt's lawful son; Evelyn's 'homage' to French Quebec, in the person of Antoinette's father, is shown to be guided by his love for Antoinette, and so secured by feminine authority.

Antoinette's two marriages present a contrast between the manly protectiveness of Evelyn and the unmanly selfishness of Sternfield; thus the novel allegorizes the contrast between military and civil government delineated in the historical summary of chapter 5. But the novel also contrasts two Antoinettes: the first, motivated by passion to defy her father and her God, and so powerless to affect her 'lord'; the second, modest, dutiful, and pious and by virtue of these qualities, authoritative in her own sphere. The novel creates Canada as the domestic space of feminine power, within which, according to the 'sexual contract,' the feminine partner has the duty and the authority to place a check upon the excesses of masculine power, and guide it according to moral laws. Antoinette's marriage to Evelyn is not acceptable merely because Evelyn shares Antoinette's Catholic faith, but because he yields to Antoinette the authority to determine matters of faith and moral behaviour, just as the British, by the novel's interpretation, 'finally accorded to Canadians the peaceful enjoyment of their institutions and their laws' (30) in yielding up domestic authority over matters of religion, education, and justice.

Thus *Antoinette de Mirecourt* is not political *in spite of* its use of romance conventions, but *because of* them. Through their use, the novel translates imperial power and colonial submission into gender, and through the fiction of the 'sexual contract' rewrites the forced submission of Canada as a relationship of equality based upon the moral authority of the oppressed feminine to limit and control the power of the oppressor. Rather than vaguely telling the story from the French-Canadian point of view, *Antoinette*, in subsuming the boundaries between political categories under gender, creates the specific authority of French Canada to write its own terms of surrender. By creating 'good and bad among both the French and the English' (MacMillan, McMullen, and Waterston 38), the novel does more than state a liberal truism; it specifically generates these moral differences within the discourse of gender in order to regulate relations between the two cultural groups.

4

Explain Yourself:
New Woman Fiction in Canada

There was only one small plot left for her to tell: the terra incognita *of herself, as she knew herself to be, not as man liked to imagine her – in a word to give herself away.*

George Egerton, 'A Keynote to Keynotes'

By the 1880s, the issue of political and social equality for women was gaining a prominent place in public discourse in Canada. The increasing visibility of violence against women within the family, a new 'scientific' discourse which located sexual desire in the female body, and the shift to women working outside the home in an industrial economy were among the factors which led women and men to question the logic of the 'sexual contract,' and to attribute to women a 'self' which domesticity seemed to proscribe. In 1883 the Toronto Women's Literary Club emerged from its benign cultural camouflage to reveal itself as a suffrage organization;[1] in the same year, Augusta Stowe-Gullen became the first female doctor to receive her education in Canada. By 1890 Sara Jeannette Duncan was calling for the vote for women in the pages of the *Toronto Globe*, and in 1892 Clara Brett Martin began her career as Ontario's first female lawyer. Prominent Canadian intellectuals such as Goldwin Smith and Andrew MacPhail offered remarks upon women's fitness for education and public office in speeches and in the pages of the *Canadian Monthly and National Review*.[2] Political agitations became the focus for a 'more broadly based nineteenth-century social crisis which was, in important respects, articulated as a crisis of definition of gender' (Pykett x); not only were some women demanding the rights previously limited to men, but such women were regarded as 'agents and symptoms of ... an insidious (ef)feminisation of the culture at large' (Pykett 9).

The New Woman novel, which took the very definition of the feminine itself as its theme, was in a manner a response to the changing status of women and to the 'general struggle about the definition of woman, and about the nature, power and function of the feminine within culture' (Pykett 10). Canadian novels of the 1890s, such as Lily Dougall's *The Madonna of a Day* (1895), Duncan's *A Daughter of Today* (1894), Maria Amelia Fytche's *Kerchiefs to Hunt Souls* (1895), and Joanna Wood's *Judith Moore* (1898) and *The Untempered Wind* (1894), as well as some later works such as Jessie Sime's *Sister Woman* (1919), show a community of interests and techniques with New Woman fiction by British and American writers such as George Egerton (Mary Chavelita Dunne), Sarah Grand, and Olive Schreiner,[3] an interest in challenging the definition of femininity according to the 'sexual contract.' The New Woman as depicted in these texts defied society by engaging in unconventional relations with men, claiming independence of movement and action, and affecting masculine dress and manners. Even her gestures are marked by her 'newness,' as she is often described as conveying discontent and restlessness in each gesture and expression, markedly contrasting the self-control and patience of the domestic ideal. Initially rejecting the social role of wife, the New Woman follows a career in the arts, business, or education; when married, she is a most unconventional wife, gently indulgent of a dull and insensitive partner or in outright rebellion against a violent, brutish, or diseased spouse. The titles of *A Daughter of Today* (1894) and *The Madonna of a Day* (1895) refer the characteristics of such feminine personalities specifically to the decade of the 1890s, suggesting that this historical period of dramatic change in the lives of women created her unstable character.

New Woman novels are usually categorized by Canadian critics as early realist works which blend the popular form of romance with 'social and sexual realism' (Gerson, *Purer Taste* 153) in detailed settings influenced by American local colourists and the form of the regional idyll (Pacey, cited in MacMillan, McMullen, and Waterston 172). According to Carrie MacMillan, such books were characterized by 'a questioning of the status quo and a looking forward to a time of female emancipation and liberation' ('Introduction' iv), and so were often rejected by the conservative gatekeepers of Canadian literary taste (Gerson, *Purer Taste* 145, 153), who associated them with materialism and immorality. Far from removing the heroine from 'a position of interest in their books which dwarfs all the other characters' (Duncan, 'Saunterings' 772), as Sara Jeannette Duncan suggested was the aim of realist depictions of female characters, New

Woman fiction used the techniques of realism to mirror the 'dramatic social changes' (MacMillan, Introduction ii) in women's lives. However, critics have noted that Canadian New Woman novels, despite their radical assertions, tended to conservative narrative resolutions which assert women's traditional desire for a husband and children. Carole Gerson attributes the contradiction between seemingly feminist and transgressive subject material yet conservative narrative forms to the authors' awareness of audience; she argues that New Woman novels 'share the problem of how to shape an unacceptable social situation into an acceptable narrative form' and solve this problem by 'resort[ing] to extraordinary devices to arrive at a printable resolution' (*Purer Taste* 146). Barbara Godard notes that in 'many novels of the 1890's ... strong feminist statements about new opportunities for women's activity clash with the endings that show conversions of these new heroines to the call of social service' ('Portrait' 89). For Carrie MacMillan, the contradiction is thematized as a 'divided self' in *Kerchiefs to Hunt Souls*, which depicts 'women who desire emancipation into the public sphere but also want heterosexual love and find that the two are often incompatible' (Introduction xii). MacMillan, McMullen, and Waterston cite the work of Rachel Blau DuPlessis on the incompatibility of *Bildung* and romance in such novels: 'these novels, it seems, are characterized by what DuPlessis describes as "the struggles between middle and ending, quest and love plots, female as hero and female as heroine"' (205).

Many critics, including Godard and MacMillan, attribute these contradictory plots and characters to an ambivalence they find inherent in feminist thought in this period. Intellectual historians have identified two major, but also contradictory, arguments in favour of women's rights commonly made in the period 1880–1920. Equal rights feminism (called by some critics, simply, feminism) held that women were entitled by right of their common humanity to equal rights with men. Maternal (or social) feminism, in contrast, grew from the North American reform movement and demanded women's rights as a tool in the fight to secure social reforms such as prohibition. Maternal feminism held that women were fundamentally different from men, and thus deserved access to specific rights (such as the vote) because they had by nature and by training 'maternal' virtues such as compassion, self-control, nurturance, compromise, and moral purity.[4] Writings by prominent feminists often used both arguments, despite the logical contradiction inherent in holding them at once. Historians and literary critics resolve this problem by suggesting, for example, that one argument represents the writer's 'real' feelings while the other is adopted as policy to persuade conservative readers: Gerson's suggestion that the authors of New Woman novels bowed to the pressure of the market-place in creating the conservative endings of their novels is an example of this approach. Alternatively, commentators suggest that women in this period may have been simply confused, unable to see that their views were logically contradictory, or ascribing that contradiction to their characters' (and their own) thwarted desire and internal psychological turmoil. New Woman novels, with their mix of radical argument and conservative narrative forms, their struggle towards 'psychological realism' and their lingering commitment to romance, seem to embody this confusion exactly (as Godard and MacMillan suggest).

However, what has been overlooked in these analyses is the clear intention of the novels themselves not to acknowledge any contradiction in their ideological perspective; instead of 'reflecting' or 'mirroring' a split between personal autonomy, and maternal self-sacrifice, these novels undertake to overcome that split, to explain it and render it invisible. These novels resignify women's struggle to define a new kind of 'self' as consistent with their newly biologically circumscribed roles as mothers of the race, and in so doing suggest that the New Woman is really the old woman, after all. Despite intermittent, seemingly feminist elements, these texts are deeply and fundamentally conservative, even in their assertion of women's sexual desire, personal autonomy, and dissatisfaction with the social institutions of marriage and motherhood.

What seem to be gaps in logic in these texts are precisely where ideology operates; the ideology of the feminine posits 'explanations' to smooth them over. By focusing on women as the problem, New Woman novels restate the hierarchy of gender by demanding that women explain themselves to an implicit reader, reinscribing the seemingly 'radical' elements of plot and character into a conservative sex/gender system. This imperative requirement to 'explain' ourselves as women is of a piece with what Foucault describes as the project of Western civilization, 'the formidable injunction to tell what one is and what one does, what one recollects and what one has forgotten ... [a]n immense labour to which the West has submitted generations in order to produce ... men's [sic] subjection: their constitution as subjects in both senses of the word' (60). In authorizing the woman to speak the mysteries of her experience of her different body, her explanation (or confession, as Foucault terms it) is also commanded by the linguistic structure which demands that she becomes stable and known. The confession of women's desire, the opening up textually of the New Woman to the gaze of 'the common reader' in order to explain and justify feminine difference, is the form of her reintegration into the discourse of the feminine, of her creation as subject to as well as subject of. 'The confession is a ritual of discourse in which the speaking subject is also the subject of the statement; it is also a ritual that unfolds within a power relationship, for one does not confess without the presence (or virtual presence) of a partner who is not simply the interlocutor but the authority who requires the confession, prescribes and appreciates it, and intervenes in order to judge, punish, forgive, console, and reconcile' (Foucault 61–2). These texts 'unfold within a power relationship' in which speaking itself does not imply power; instead, in these texts 'explanation is a form of subjugation' (Ladha 59). New Woman fiction thus does less to free women from stereotypes than it does to reify the power relationship between men and women by responding to the imperative to explain, to speak, to justify women, and therefore to reinsert them into the hierarchy of gender.

The ideological project of revealing and so refiguring femininity within the hierarchy of gender was understood within the discourse of art as a product of the *fin de siècle*. The culture of the *fin de siècle* was held to be exhausted, and artists at a loss for material, searching out the extreme and the exotic as the only subject material left unappropriated by previous generations. This search for the new and unrepresented, whether it be exotic foreign lands or the unknown interior life of woman, was often expressed in metaphors drawn from science. Following the French realists, English New Woman authors figured their project in writing novels as a scientific one which involved the researching and representation of unknown or undiscovered aspects of material life for the moral education of their readers. George Egerton describes her fiction using metaphors of cartography: feminine experience is a 'terra incognita' to be explored and mapped for readers. Medical metaphors of dissection and examination were also common: 'In the imaginative as well as the medical literature of the *fin de siècle*, the woman becomes the case study as well as the case, an object to be incisively opened, analysed, and reassembled' (Showalter, *Sexual Anarchy* 128). In both of these metaphorical constructions, however, Woman is represented as the unknown and passive *materiel* to be explored by the artist, whose action in exploring is masculine; thus these cultural metaphors inscribe the split subjectivity of the woman writer who, in taking herself as theme of her work, is both subject of her discourse and subject to it.

In the final decades of the nineteenth century, the discourse of inductive science 'spoke with the imperious tone of a discipline newly claiming, and in large measure being granted, decisive authority in matters social as well as strictly scientific' (Russett 3–4). Using principles such as biogenetic law, sexual selection, the conservation of energy, and the physiological division of labour,[5] turn-of-the-century scientists reinscribed the gender hierarchy as arising directly from human biology and thus not only morally defensible but physically unavoidable, reconfining the feminine to an even smaller sphere than domesticity. For scientific thinkers in the 1880s and '90s, 'women's sexual organs, rather than being a part of the whole, were virtually the whole' (Mitchinson, *The Nature* 31), and women's reproductive role and its supposed effects upon her physical and mental development determined the authentic feminine self. Any woman who failed to recognize this 'fact' was doomed to be literally ungendered by the withering and eventual loss of her sexual and reproductive capacity: unmarried, childless women were thought to be unsexed. Scientific thought reduced feminine practice to recognition and acceptance of women's only responsible social role, that of reproduction; feminine authority was no longer based on women's conscious knowledge of their own sphere and their agency in governing that sphere through self-control, modesty, and frugality, but on their biological and instinctual identification with Woman. 'Science, then, can be seen as a weapon used by men to rationalize the perpetuation of traditional sex roles and men's continued domination of women' (Russett 191). In the scientific discourse of the time, women were and must be feminine, even against their own wills; any attempt to oppose the narrative of sexual science merely proved its overwhelming necessity.

As Penny Boumelha notes in *Thomas Hardy and Women*, this newly defined ideology of 'womanhood' (as opposed to the earlier domestic 'womanliness') is a conservative response to the destabilizing force of first-wave feminism, a backlash that encloses women even more closely: 'womanhood, in contrast to womanliness, is not an ideal or an aspiration, but an immanent natural disposition, originating in a pre-determining physiological sexual differentiation ... It draws much of its strength from its protest against the existing social oppression of woman, but it subverts that protest by an appeal to the "natural" which reinforces the enclosure of women's experience by their physiological organization' (85–6). Just as leaving off corsets contradictorily further restricted women's liberty by demanding that their actual bodies conform to a prescribed shape, so the shucking of the ideal garb of domestic 'womanliness,' rather than increasing women's freedom to define themselves, prescribed an even more limited set of supposedly biological norms essential to the feminine self, and redefined deviation from them as a deviation from nature. Thus, women who denied 'nature' in the pursuit of social and political advances for women are represented as inherently false and untrustworthy, for in denying their biological drive to have children and submit themselves to male authority/protection, they are denying an authentic inner self motivated primarily to procreate within a heterosexual family. In these books, women are feminine in spite of themselves; the only practice accepted as evidence of inner gender is the eventual acceptance by the female characters of their own reproductive and maternal potential.[6]

Because concepts of the natural were so important in socio-scientific discourse, Canada served a special function in the assumption of a biological womanhood in Canadian New Woman fiction. Sometimes unproblematically identified with the natural, or more often as the space where nature meets culture, Canada becomes for many writers a feminine space where, domestic 'womanliness' already discarded, 'womanhood' can be discovered and understood. *Judith Moore* and *The Untempered Wind*, by Joanna Wood, and *The Madonna of a Day*, by Lily Dougall, are examples of texts from late-nineteenth-century Canada which use an identification between womanhood and the natural world to reconfine the New Woman within the bounds of a biologically defined femininity.

Joanna Wood's *Judith Moore; or, Fashioning a Pipe* depicts a New Woman heroine who discovers her natural womanhood in an idyllic agricultural settlement in Canada. Judith Moore is the 'pipe' referred to in the subtitle, for like an instrument she makes her living by singing. Yet the strain of her public career upon her 'nervous organization' threatens her with complete physical collapse; only through recovering her womanhood in a traditional romance with the rustic swain Andrew Coward can she be restored to health. The novel ends as her new husband forbids her to sing in public, and she happily acquiesces.[7] Despite the heroine's independence and successful international career, characteristics which mark her as a New Woman, the parable of *Judith Moore* merely rewrites the 'old woman' of the domestic ideal as the authentic self which masquerades as a career artist. The narrator describes Judith as 'the woman of the past, the woman who created a "type" distinct from man; the womanly woman, not the hybrid creature of modern cultivation; the woman of romance' (97).

While *Judith Moore* represents a woman's career in realistic detail, it draws upon the 'biogenetic law' and the theory of the 'conservation of energy' to develop in the title character a version of biological womanhood. According to the biogenetic law, 'ontogeny recapitulates phylogeny' (Russett 50), that is, the development of each individual human is supposed to recapitulate the history of human evolution. By this theory, women are considered to be undeveloped men, frozen forever at the adolescent stage of their development while the remainder of their energy is used to support reproduction. The theory of the conservation of energy reinforced biogenetic law, by suggesting that developmental energies are finite, and if women used theirs to progress past the stage of adolescence to individual maturity (which is by definition masculine), they jeopardize their ability to reproduce and risk becoming sterile. The narrator of *Judith Moore* comments that Judith has only narrowly escaped this fate: 'Had she been less evenly balanced, had her soul been less true, her heart less tender, she might in time have frozen the woman completely, and crystallised into the *artiste* only' (96). Andrew, the 'countryman' who is 'so different from the artificial creatures she had known' (101), gives Judith the opportunity to recover her authentic self by falling in love with her and offering her a role as wife and mother.

Andrew is a farmer and hunter, a man who both nurtures and controls the natural world. His family association with Old World culture in conjunction with his competence as a farmer marks him as the 'classless' Canadian man idealized in much turn-of-the-century Canadian fiction, prosperous and educated, yet physically active and an accomplished workman. His role in the novel is to understand and revive Judith's 'womanhood,' just as he understands his land and its potential to bring forth. He hears 'that mute appeal of nature to be understood – like some sweet woman, smitten into a spell of suffering silence, till such time as the magic word shall release her. A word she knows, yet cannot, of her own power, speak' (57). Andrew speaks the word for her and releases her into identity with a gendered self which is essentially passive and reproductive – relieving her of the obligation to perform in public and allowing her to feel the biological urge towards reproduction and heterosexual union, which the novel presents as distorted by her career. 'She had never before been considered as a woman, but always as a singer; and her womanhood recognizing the tribute paid to it, stirred into life, responded to the feeling which evoked it, and demanded right of way' (157).

The characterization of Judith's singing is central to her representation as feminine. Her talent is presented as a natural outcome of her feminine emotions, rather than the result of education, hard work, or ambition. 'This was in reality the great charm of Judith's singing – a charm no perfection of method, no quality of tone could have produced. She felt the full significance of everything she sang, and had that sympathetic magnetism which creates its own moods in others. That is fascination' (108–9). Judith's singing is a result of her feminine ability to feel emotion, and the 'sympathetic magnetism' of sexual fascination. Like a pipe, Judith creates music through the action of her breath, by 'inhal[ing] the common ether of a prosaic world, mingl[ing] it with her breath, and sen[ding] it forth glorified as sound' (93). Thus her singing is a natural effect of her body's existence, and has its organic function in expressing her femininity. Her singing is an attribute of her sex and has its natural audience – Andrew, who instinctively removes his hat when he first hears her song across the fields. Judith's song is identified both with sacredness and with the Sirens (14), and like the domestic feminine ideal has the social function of elevating men's minds towards God as well as attracting a potential mate. Thus Judith's voice is constructed as a kind of secondary sex characteristic, an element of attraction between men and women and a proof of her gender.

The novel uses the contrast between Judith's voice heard in private and public settings in order to further confine feminine 'nature' to private space. Heard across the open fields in the settlement of Ovid, Judith's singing is a pure expression of her feminine self. However, the novel differentiates this experience from singing for profit, in public, which changes the demands made on her body and her emotions. Judith's sensitive emotional organization cannot stand the stress of performing in public: 'the world had crowned her great – Fools who could not see that the head they crowned was already drooping beneath its lonely burden' (29). Judith is unable to bear the emotional and physical stress of performance because 'when she returned to earth, there was no loving breast for her to rest upon, no strong hands to sustain her, no lips to kiss the pain of music from her own, none to seal the bliss of singing into abiding joy' (94). Her lack of a lover causes an 'imbalance' between her mental and physical make-up; 'the rarefied air which solitary success breathes' (96) has caused her to leave behind the 'Happy Valley' (96) of physical and emotional fulfilment.

Like the pipes of Pan referred to in the novel's subtitle, Judith suffers cruel deformation of her nature in order to create music in the commercial world beyond her own hearth and home. In the lengthy quote from Elizabeth Barrett Browning's poem which begins the novel, Pan 'hacked and hewed ... with his hard bleak steel' and 'drew the pith, like the heart of a man,' from the reed he selected to make his pipe. The narrator of the novel comments: 'The "Great God Pan" was all unconscious of his cruelty, was he not, when he fashioned the pipe out of a river reed? And as he blew through it the music of the gods, doubtless had good reason for thinking that never reed had been honoured like unto this reed' (30). Like Pan's reed, Judith stands in danger of becoming physically and mentally deformed by singing for public audiences. The novel creates womanhood and the career of an artist as opposites, in much the same way that *Roughing It in the Bush* opposes domesticity and a literary career, suggesting that success in one venue must mean leaving the other far behind.

In Joanna Wood's first novel, *The Untempered Wind*, the biological and reproductive 'nature' of the central character, Myron Holder, is similarly presented as both authentic and overwhelming. The most striking element of the characterization of Myron is the account of her wild and secret run through the countryside at night, which associates her own 'nature' with the landscape: 'As she ran, the spirit of the night and the intoxicating odor of flowers and grasses entered into her and steeped her senses in a delirium of freedom' (229). This vision of freedom in the natural world is reinforced by Myron's belief that the promise she exchanged with the father of her illegitimate child, 'under no more sacred canopy than the topaz of a summer sky – with no other bridal hymn than the choral of the wind among the trees' (6), is as sacred, if not more so, than a conventional marriage. Yet despite the discourse of desire which expresses Myron's sexual encounter, her action is also constructed as being 'in obedience to ... the voice of nature' (6), which is represented as an inner compulsion towards heterosexual sex and reproduction. The novel's representation of the unwed mother as both wilful and obedient, morally innocent yet needing to be 'tempered' through suffering, is only contradictory on the surface: 'nature,' represented as both irresistibly pleasurable and inexorably mechanical, is the ideological complex which resolves these issues.

The Methodist townsfolk of Jamestown, like many other inhabitants of small towns in Canadian fiction,[8] are quick to condemn Myron's sexual encounter when an illegitimate child appears. Myron's suffering in disgrace is metaphorically linked to the suffering of both Christ and His Mother for the sin of human passion. But Myron dedicates herself to a life of service and submits to the judgment of a Christian minister that she must declare her sinfulness to each new acquaintance. Her disruptive 'delirium of freedom' is contained, both by her recognition of its sinfulness and her turn to self-sacrifice in response, and by her continued faithfulness to the promise of sexual fidelity she entered into with the father of her child. She finally marries her son's father on her deathbed.

The novel treats Myron's plight, as a single mother isolated and shunned by her neighbours, with sympathy, and both the townsfolk and the father of her child are condemned for causing her and her innocent son needless suffering. In the tradition of the problem novel, it suggests that Myron should have been treated with Christian charity by the towns-folk and by the Church, and with fidelity and integrity by her lover, but it does not suggest that Myron in any way expressed individual agency and desire in her deviation from the norm, nor does it advocate such devia-tion. Rather, it represents Myron as acting in obedience to nature by breaking an 'artificial law' (7) and thus becoming a victim of an unfaith-ful man. The novel argues that the man ought to have been faithful, and Myron's condition pitied, not that Myron or other women should be able to transgress such 'laws' at will. Myron's 'authentic self,' meek, enduring, and defined by the element of self-sacrifice for her child, is a most con-ventional one, despite the lapse from strict chastity which a morally neu-tral 'nature' commanded.

In opposition to this increasingly materialist view of women's role, thinkers such as Lily Dougall emphasized women's traditional association with self-control and thus with altruism, morality, and religious belief. Distaining a merely material explanation of human life, such thinkers attributed the feminine 'inner self' to a Nature informed by the divine. Such a feminine self functioned not merely to reproduce, but to present an ideal to motivate human striving, an example of charity and self-sacrifice to make human life more bearable, and a vision of weakness and innocence to motivate male altruism. As in the materialist model, women are intimately associated with Nature, though a nature informed by God; as in the materialist model, women are confined to a sphere of comple-mentarity with men, whereby they come to recognize their authentic selves in service and self-sacrifice. While the 'spiritual' model of feminin-ity claims a measure of freedom from biological determinism, it is also compatible with it, for it considers the feminine role determined by the obsolete 'sexual contract' to be both the product of and the motivation for social evolution.

The natural world, defined as both Canadian wilderness landscape and the primitive conditions of human society in that landscape, is the means whereby the heroine of Lily Dougall's *The Madonna of a Day* is brought to acknowledge her authentic self and its essential femininity. The novel refers to the popularly held belief, an outgrowth of the theory of recapit-ulation, that societies in which women are most idealized are the most advanced. The novel creates a so-called wilderness society of miners in the Rockies who have degenerated[9] from the heights of civilization because they have no women. The heroine, Mary Howard, comes to understand that women's physical weakness necessitates an idealized moral and spiritual Womanhood; only by striving to embody innocence, piety, and dependence is she able to rouse the chivalrous protectiveness of men. Mary's presence, and the men's attempts to protect her from injury and rape, cause a moral renovation of uncivilized male souls and necessitate Mary's own acknowledgment that her despised femininity is both socially necessary and 'natural.'

Mary Howard initially identifies herself as a New Woman: 'I am "emancipated," I am "advanced," in fact I am the "new woman," so far as she is not a myth' (17), she provocatively declares to a missionary whom she meets on the CPR. She is agnostic, independent, and makes her own living; she claims many men as friends and abhors love-making and affectionate sentiment, representing herself as 'one of the fellows' and an equal to her male friends. But even Mary knows that such freedoms have not changed the feminine essence created by evolution: she protests to her missionary friend, 'Now, do you suppose that evolution has suddenly come to a standstill, and that a new thing has been created?' (15). Her safe passage around the world and the courteous treatment she receives at the hands of men is based, not on their ability to see her as a comrade, but on their respect for her as a woman. When she falls from the train at night in the Rockies, in deep snow miles from any station, her attention is forcibly returned to that femininity which was created by 'nature'; in this setting, she learns that her 'natural' feminine self is not 'imperious and indomitable' but 'gentle and fearful' (29). In the course of her struggle to gain food and shelter, and to avoid marriage with the leader of the miners, she discovers that the relationship between women and men can be one of power and violence, if women allow their moral purity to be compromised by rejecting their role as moral guardians. Mary no longer sees herself as 'one of the fellows' and begins to understand that her vulnerability to male violence demands that she see herself as a woman: 'she began to have a sensation that the ground of all her lifelong security was slipping from beneath her feet' (181). In this natural setting, her only defence is the men's instinctive reverence for 'the eternal sanctity of young and beautiful womanhood,' (34), and indeed her natural function is to embody 'their ideal, such inarticulate undefined ideal as they had' (37).

The material world is constructed as Mary's teacher in her return to a spiritual and idealist conception of womanhood. Mary experiences a sense that 'her mind lifted into a different class of thoughts and sensations' (55) when she contemplates the incongruity of a 'mountain peak that was monarch of them all ... a vast monument of such transcendent

beauty' set in 'this bleak chaotic place' (55–6). She comes to the conclusion that 'the mountain sang of an inspiration toward an impossible perfection, the struggle for which was the joy, the only joy, of the universe'
(59).[10] She concludes from this that her social role must be to embody
that perfection for the miners, for 'perfect nobleness of character alone'
is sacred to them, and will motivate them to spare her life (71). She
comes to articulate such an ideal within the context of the worldliness
and vulgar selfishness that was her previous life: 'women ... would give up
their foolish pastimes and come to places like this, and just be gentle, and
good and true, and merry in their own way ... reading story books and
poems, and having the fear of God always in their faces' (197). Her own
embodiment of the transcendent ideal of woman, its helplessness, purity,
and sacred maternal function, shines forth in the midst of the chaotic
and barbaric community she encounters. And only when she feels her
gentleness, dependence, and moral purity in an unalienated way is she
able to call forth the best instincts of the men; her attempts to feign
moral piety and Christian belief merely convince them of her duplicity,
and so justify their own violence and duplicity. Their ideal of her tends to
make her good or, at least, provides the motivation for her to try to be
good: 'The power this man's ideal of her had over him transcended her
vainest wish, and she saw herself to be base ... The thought that, if she had
chosen, she might have been the noble woman that he supposed her
to be was intolerable' (245). In the final chapter of the novel, Mary
Howard's confusion over her experience prompts her to debate women's
social role with the missionary. She reiterates, 'I do not believe in the little humdrum rules and regulations that men make for women' (260–1),
yet the missionary confirms that despite the legal rights that women have
acquired in the nineteenth century 'there is need that women should still
conform to this same ideal' (266), the ideal of moral transcendence
through self-control and self-sacrifice. 'It is this holy ideal reflected in
good women that men worship in such sort that they can subdue selfishness in its presence. Without it ... nothing can save you from becoming
the victim of man's selfishness, because he is stronger than you' (264–5).
The vision of gradual progress through inheritance, expressed in the
natural world in which 'the living trees had been sown upon their fallen
progenitors' (61), implies the importance of women's role in the social
evolution of humanity towards altruism and peace; they must act according to the 'nature' God made for them.

According to Gillian Beer, the concept of evolution had an inordinate
impact on the novel, for 'topics traditional to the novel – courtship, sensi-

bility, the making of matches, women's beauty, men's dominance, *inheritance* in all its forms – became charged with new difficulty in the wake of the publication of *The Descent of Man*' (213). The traditional themes of romance were no longer the stuff of mere stories, but the ingredients which went into making the future of humanity. In this narrative, women's role was essentially passive: though Darwin admitted that in most species the female chose her own mate, in humans, he argued, the male's superior strength (and intelligence) meant that he chose. Thus romance plots, as directed by turn-of-the-century thought, required that women remain the objects of narrative desire by recognizing and conforming to their 'natural' role, a position which was in conflict with the movement for women's social and political rights.

The role of heredity in the formation of personality becomes a focus of fictional narrative in Maria Amelia Fytche's *Kerchiefs to Hunt Souls*. Dorothy Pembroke, like Mary Howard, also comes to embrace a femininity whose task is to improve the race through intelligent sexual selection; while she may be 'unduly interested in and familiar with sexual feeling' (Pykett 140), such feeling is attributable to her biological inheritance and ultimately leads her to the appropriate mate. If in the New Woman novel the practices of the domestic woman are rejected as 'shamming' (Dougall 14), the redefinition of femininity as instrumental in evolution created a form of feminine inner self which needed no evidence.

The novel begins as Dorothy Pembroke rejects Harry Alexander's proposal of marriage. Harry is rich, educated, devoted, and witty, as well as being Dorothy's best friend, who supports her 'advanced' political views and her career as a teacher. But what Dorothy wants is a grand sexual passion; she wants to travel the world in order to discover her 'affinity,' the other half of her own soul, according to a popular late-Victorian metaphor of heterosexual desire, and she has planned a trip to Europe in order to search for love and life experience. Her rejection of Alexander creates the enigma to be revealed: is the passion Dorothy craves possible, or even desirable, as a basis for lifelong commitment? The novel concludes that such passions are merely kerchiefs to hunt souls (Ezekiel 13:18), vain imaginings that distract from the truth.

Dorothy Pembroke is a New Woman; head of a school for young ladies, she is also an 'advanced' thinker, playfully associated by Alexander with all the fashionably progressive issues of the 1890s, an 'advocate for woman suffrage and emancipation, for equal opportunities for smoking, drinking, flirting and loving, boating, muscular Christianity, high-church sisterhoods, Salvation Army parades, and Christian Science' (7). However, she retains a vision of romantic attachment which is clearly idealist: 'I believe that I am but the incomplete half of an immortal being, and that in heaven, though they neither marry nor are given in marriage, two affinities in this world will be joined ... I feel my incompleteness here more than I can express; all my aspirations seem to fall short of the mark. I shall wait till I meet my affinity before I marry' (8–9).[11] Dorothy is perfectly prepared to remain single should she be unable to locate her affinity: 'Marriage, thank goodness, is not the aim and end of woman's life in this nineteenth century,' she says (9). However, the narrator makes clear that her desire for a grand passion is chimerical, and has its source in her romantic education (287–8) and in her inheritance of an unstable personality from her violently evangelical parents: 'Was it a relic of her father's conservatism and orthodoxy, or was it religious fanaticism mingled with romance, inherited from her mother, that made her such a devout believer in old-fashioned love?' (43) the text asks.

The theme of the importance of biological inheritance, made popular by the French naturalist authors, is reiterated in the story of Harry Alexander, a survivor of a love match with the daughter of an alcoholic army chaplain. Now a widower and father of an 'idiot' son, Alexander attributes the failure of his marriage to heredity. 'It is to the emotional love-matches that we are indebted for the idiots, epileptics, and criminals' (8), he argues, in an attempt to persuade Dorothy to accept him. His argument is proved correct when Dorothy's 'affinity,' Gaston, leaves her to marry the wife chosen for him by his mother. Gaston is a 'fils de Gaulois' (243), and, consistent with nineteenth-century racial attitudes, his French inheritance makes him mercurial, mercenary, and deferential to his mother and the Catholic Church. This inheritance dictates that he will abandon the bride he married in a British civil ceremony without his parents' consent. He identifies her as his 'Psyche,' his soul, confirming Dorothy's belief in affinities, yet their marriage is a disaster as he proves to be her Mercury, easily swayed and changeable.

To the extent that *Kerchiefs to Hunt Souls* addresses social issues, it does so by purporting to reveal information about conditions of life for single women, information which is constructed as shrouded in the secrecy of decorum and reputation. Dorothy's experiences as a naïve young woman in search of work exemplify the various snares laid for the educated and beautiful woman; her friendship with Alice Jefferies reveals the problems of those with little education and no looks. Like Jessie Sime's *Sister Woman*, the novel provides information about abuses of servants and governesses by their wealthy employers and by the charitable homes they patronize, offering an inside view of the lives of women in the English community in Paris. It self-consciously crusades for better treatment for servants and governesses, and also purports to represent the Parisian view of American forwardness and vulgarity, again revealing knowledge hidden by barriers of language, culture, and class.

Kerchiefs to Hunt Souls thus 'explains' Dorothy's rejection of Alexander by heredity: her biology and its effect upon her ability to make decisions is the secret which the novel reveals by proving her desire for sexual passion to be chimerical. This 'explanation' is supplemented by the novel's description of her inadequate education and the loveless atmosphere and exploitative conditions of women's employment, which encourage such dreams and the hopes of their realization. Thus the novel is progressive to the extent that it attributes part of Dorothy's failure to the social conditions of women's existence, but it also shows her to be even more surely confined by biology, an immutable 'natural' element of women's existence which renders all of women's attempts to make free choices useless.

The shift from a socially defined ideal of the domestic 'sexual contract' to the evolutionary 'womanhood' evidenced in these examples privileges the female writer, who could now claim direct authority to write out feminine experience. The location of feminine experience within the biological female body 'predicates certain kinds of experience as female, and in doing so it privileges the interiority of the female writer and, in turn, of the female narrative voice' (Boumelha 86). Thus, in describing 'The Novel of the Modern Woman,' W.T. Stead specifies that such novels are written only by women: 'The Modern Woman novel is not merely a novel written by a woman, or a novel written about women, but it is a novel written by a woman about women from the standpoint of Woman' (64). The authority thus granted to women writers in the redefinition of Woman was certainly an advance for women in material terms; it allowed many women to have literary careers and incomes. However, in order to speak, women must enter into a discourse which figures them as object, as problem, as mystery to be revealed and solved, which therefore creates them as subject to as well as subject of their own enunciation. By accepting the problematization of woman as a category, these books acquiesce in a power structure in which woman is the subordinate term.

This hierarchy is inscribed in the common formulation of gender issues at the turn of the century by the phrase 'woman question.' This 'question' is often vague: 'What do women want?' or 'What should the social position of women be?' However, in order to determine why woman should be a 'question' all, it is necessary to discover who asks the woman question, and who answers. The New Woman novel often self-consciously presents itself as a response to this question, and foregrounds the circumstances of its asking. The Prologue to Jessie Sime's *Sister Woman* dramatizes the situation which is the beginning point of all of these novels – a man complains, 'You women don't know what you want,' and suggests that the narrator 'be articulate' (7) in order to explain women's lives to him. The narrator responds by creating the vignettes of character and action which explain women to her male hearer.[12] The fact that the question is asked of woman implies her authority to answer; but it also suggests the power of the male examiner, who listens and in the end pronounces dismissively: 'Then that's the lot' (292). As Jane Tompkins remarks, 'The impassivity of male silence suggests the inadequacy of female verbalization, establishes male superiority, and silences the one who would engage in conversation' (*West* 59).

This does not necessarily imply that all New Woman novels self-consciously address a male reader: the majority of readers of these novels were female. However, the novels exist as a reply to an implicit demand of patriarchy, to 'be articulate' within the bounds set by patriarchal language. In Jessie Sime's *Sister Woman*, the male listener is made explicit: the main action is framed by a question posed by a man, and its narration is explicitly an answer to the question. The Prologue to *Sister Woman* ends as the woman journalist 't[akes] the cover off [her] typewriter and s[its] down before it ...' (8). Thus the collection of twenty-eight stories which follows is offered as a reply to the man's command: 'State your grievance' (8). The stories are marked as New Woman fiction immediately as the protagonist of the opening story, 'Alone,' a housekeeper who has chosen to live secretly as her employer's lover, prepares to make their relationship public by expressing her grief at his death. Many of the stories recount such 'irregular unions' of married men and their mistresses, or single men and their employees who choose not to marry, and some involve illegitimate children. Most focus on women who work for a living, though they differ from much New Woman writing in including the experience of working-class women and prostitutes as well as the middle-class 'business woman' (secretary). These stories, however, insist that despite the newness of the style of life chosen by some of the protagonists, and the sordid details of exploitation endured by others, the biological 'womanhood' of the women described remains eternal, unchanging, and essentially defined by their roles as heterosexual lovers, caregivers, and mothers.

Several of the stories describe women who, despite life choices which are presented as unconventional, still conform to the domestic ideal. The protagonist of 'Alone' falls in love with her employer as she invests more

and more of her emotional life in her job as his housekeeper. 'The fold-
ing his clothes, the putting them away, the little mendings and darnings
that she used to do for him ... she remembered that sometimes she was
puzzled at her joy in doing them. There was something new in all of it;
and yet, behind, somewhere, it all felt infinitely old' (13). The 'joy' she
feels in something 'infinitely old' is a result of her natural desire to perform the role of domestic help to a 'good man,' a desire which, the stories make clear, is common to all women, not just those who choose
Domestic Science as a career. As Sime herself argued, 'the central desire
of the normal woman is to please some one of whom she is fond, and the
more normal she is, the more will that desire occupy the inmost place in
her heart' (cited in Campbell xxv). In 'An Irregular Union,' Phyllis Red-
mayne, 'the ubiquitous Business Girl of our time' (76), sees her relationship to her employer as exactly comparable to that of a wife: 'For all that
was unexpected in her ideas, her typewriter might just as well have been a
kitchen stove – or a cradle. She looked on Dick Radcliffe as Eve looked on
Adam. She thought the same old things that women always have thought,
though she gained her own living and imagined she was independent
and free and modern and all the rest of it' (78). While Phyllis takes no
money from Dick for her services as his mistress, a circumstance which
she feels guards her independence, 'there are moments when she almost
certainly does want' (79) to be his wife.

  'Love-O-Man' addresses the issue of sexual desire in women, offering a
narrative of feminine life in which the characteristics of a universal
Woman in individual women are awakened by intense sexual love and/or
the birth of a child. Elsie, an elderly Scots cook, explains to the narrator
that now that her husband is dead and her child married, she looks forward to a reunion (in this life or the next) with her true love, Jamie,
whose intense sexual love made her a woman. 'Ye'll mind ... how the
woman sleeps i' ye at the first ...?' asks Elsie of the narrator, and goes on
to explain how the experience of childbirth wakens the 'mither 'at sleeps
i' the lassie' (50) for some women, but that for other women, 'it's the
sweetness o' whit the man has tae gi'e her' (51) that awakens her knowledge of herself. Elsie calls upon the narrator to own the truth of her
words as common to all women: 'gin woman meets wi' woman, mem,
she'll clash o' whit lies neist her heart ... and ther's nae eddication'll
stand atwixt the twa o' them' (53). The narrator confirms Elsie's reliance
upon an essential womanhood by referring to the 'eternal feminine way'
(53) they share. As Sandra Campbell has argued, this 'gynocentric dialogue transcends differences in ages, education, ethnic origin and social

status' ('Introduction' ix), but at the expense of reducing women to their heterosexual reproductive and sexual histories.

Motherhood is the third eternal in feminine behaviour which the stories address. In 'Jaquot and Pierre,' a childless woman laments, 'How strange is this longing that we have for children! ... Life is an empty thing without a child. Life is without reason if one has not got a child' (111–12). In 'The Child' and 'Motherhood,' the love of the protagonists for their illegitimate children changes their lives, giving them renewed ambition and a sense of self-worth. In 'A Page from Life,' a childless woman greets the son her husband unexpectedly brings home from the orphanage: 'My child, my child ... have ye come to me, have ye come at last?' (199). Even Donna, the elegant and aimless protagonist of 'A Social Problem,' feels a desire for a baby (215).

While stories such as 'A Social Problem' and the familiar anthology piece 'Munitions!' suggest that women need productive work and are strong enough and capable enough to enjoy it, *Sister Woman* reiterates the theme that despite the social changes implied by these narratives, Woman herself is eternal and unchanging, and marked by an innate desire for union with a man, love of domestic life, and a drive to have children. The stories accommodate the practices of sexual relations outside of marriage, of women's desire for careers and productive work, and of sexually expressive behaviour in women to an inner self who is biologically determined to be mate and mother. The 'Epilogue' expresses the male hearer's 'relief' that women's desire 'sounds simple' (292); the act of articulating the feminine self has allowed the male hearer to objectify and contain women's desire in predictable and traditional forms. While the narrator attempts to evade this containment by protesting, 'I'm not even started yet' (292), the collection ends here; though the last words of the 'Epilogue' describe an action performed by the narrator, in a sense, the man has had the last word.

While these texts refer to practices which are in many ways feminist, they construct such practices as ephemeralities in evolutionary time and signify as 'real' a radically conservative view of the feminine inner self. Like the French naturalists, they draw upon popular understandings of heredity and evolution to signify humans as primarily material beings whose essence is determined by their biology and their physical conditions of life. By signifying as real the feminine self as constructed by science, they grant authority only to those aspects of femininity which are authorized by biological and evolutionary theories, that is, to those aspects of femininity which define woman as the sex whose legitimate social function is repro-

duction. Significant dissent from this position harks back to domestic ideology by constructing women as idealized guardians of spiritual ideals in
an increasingly materialist society. While New Woman fiction represents
the dramatic social changes of this period in the actions of female characters, it also represents these changes as ephemeral, a distraction from the
eternal and unchanging inner self of women.

In taking the definition of Woman herself as its focus, and in laying bare
the mysteries of Woman to the penetrating gaze of the reader, New
Woman fiction inscribes itself in the gender hierarchy as the subordinate
term and marks itself as feminine textual practice. In purporting to
'explain' woman, these texts implicitly acknowledge the authority of patriarchy and respond to its demand that Woman remain the ultimate object
of both knowledge and narrative. In adopting the metaphors and the discourse of evolutionary and biological science of the turn of the century,
New Woman texts like *Judith Moore, The Untempered Wind, The Madonna of a
Day, Kerchiefs to Hunt Souls,* and *Sister Woman* redefine and reconfine
women in the role of passive partner in heterosexual reproduction with a
relentless and predictable reiterative force. Rather than representing a
step into a liberatory narrative of subjective agency, they reiterate women's
subjection to linguistic norms.

5

Voicing the Voiceless: The Practice of 'Self-expression' in Nellie McClung's Fiction and Her Autobiography

Haven't I towld ye time out of mind that a soft answer turns away wrath, and for-bye makes them madder than anything ye could say to them?

Nellie McClung, *Sowing Seeds in Danny*

The emergent 'biological' womanhood of New Woman novels did not extinguish the discourses of domesticity; rather, practices authorized by domestic ideology survived to be incorporated into a contradictory view of woman as both sexual and self-sacrificing, driven towards reproduction yet the natural check on masculine desire, rightly able to perform both domestic work and work for pay (often at the same time). This form of the feminine ideal was modified in the early twentieth century in Canada by intersection with the discourse of democratic individualism in the work of suffrage activitist Nellie McClung. McClung's fiction and her autobiography dramatize this intersection in order to resolve it themati-cally and formally through the practice of feminine 'self-expression.' In her essay 'The Writer's Creed,' McClung 'argued that "the greatest thing an author can do is to teach human beings self-expression – without which life is changed from a well-rivered landscape into a pestilential swamp"' (cited in Hallett and Davis 222). Her fiction and her autobiogra-phy represent the theme of self-expression for women, creating female characters who learn to 'speak out' despite the abusive power of men to silence them, and whose speaking in itself is both justified feminine prac-tice and significant political action which works to aid women in their struggle for social and political equality. Yet the concept of self-expres-sion as politically progressive is a problematic one, as the New Woman novels suggest; self-expression relies upon a concept of a natural self which reinstals the stereotypes of the feminine which it seeks to over-throw, and 'speaking out' comes to be demanded by a coercive power structure which seeks to control the unknown by forcing it into linguistic categories. While McClung's writing suggests the power to reverse and resignify the feminine which can be gained through linguistic subjectiv-ity, these stories also represent the contradictory nature of self-actualiza-tion and consequently of self-expression as a political strategy.

McClung's novels in themselves constitute a form of 'speaking out' within the literary discourse of the novel by generating and articulating a concept of the real which they use to challenge literary and generic con-ventions. The novels appeal to reality in order to discard conventional rep-resentations of women in rural life and in stories of romantic love, and to comment on and modify the narrative convention of the happy ending which typically closes popular stories. In addition, McClung's autobiogra-phies create a feminine self which challenges the generic requirements of autonomy, uniqueness, and public importance by appealing to a concept of feminine nature generated by the discourse of domesticity. Yet the appeal to reality or nature to justify these departures from literary conven-tion has the effect of generating a new and universal 'nature' which is as confining as the outworn stereotypes it is meant to replace.

Nellie McClung is best known in Canada today for her role as an activist in the women's movement of the early twentieth century. A major theorist of maternal feminism, McClung argued for women's suffrage and in-creased opportunities for women in public life on the basis of her strong identification with patriarchally defined domestic femininity, concluding that if women really are more moral, more self-sacrificing, and more nur-turing than men, they should by rights have authority over those aspects of public policy which fall within their area of expertise, including welfare, the family, public health, and public morality. Whether this position was a strategy adopted by canny leaders like McClung to make the revisioning of women's role more acceptable to a conservative population,[1] or whether maternal feminism was a strongly held belief, is a matter of contention among feminist scholars, as is the designation of such views as feminist at all.[2] If Nellie McClung sought to 'legitimize women's entry into the pubic sphere by comparing politics to a house in need of spring cleaning' (Val-verde 28) in accordance with the domestic ideal, she also called upon the discourse of democratic individualism to argue that women and men were 'different but equal' and therefore should have equal political rights (Prentice et al. 199).

This fracture in maternal feminist ideology reproduces what some have identified as a central theme in Canadian thought, the struggle to reconcile liberal self-actualization with membership in a moral community.[3] To some extent this contradiction is resolved in McClung's essays, stories, and novels by social (United Church) Christianity, in which the self is actualized through self-sacrifice and community service. Similarly, the contradiction generated by liberal ideology between the self and domesticity is embedded, in McClung's fiction, in a concept of a feminine self who is herself constructed by the domestic virtues of self-control, self-sacrifice, and membership in a moral community.

McClung's role as an activist and propagandist for maternal feminism has often overshadowed her career as a writer of popular fiction, where the issues raised by her politics are placed in contention and offered resolution through the structure of narrative closure. This practice of self-expression, by the texts and by their characters, engages the controversies surrounding maternal feminism by asserting that women have unique selves to be expressed which are intrinsically interesting; what they express is thus not the essential nature of the feminine, but personal and individuated experience which is partly the experience of biological sex. McClung's texts oppose the generalizing science which in the New Woman novels suggests that women who achieve individual maturity are not feminine, and that each woman, because less individuated, is more representative of her sex than her self; while they do consider biology a defining element of femininity, they draw on liberal ideology to assert women's equality as individuals with men.

The barriers to self-expression in a society organized according to masculine concerns are the thematic focus of many of McClung's fictions. In her stories and novels, women are silent partners in the project of pioneer life, the conquest of the wilderness and the provision of material wealth, contributing their labour without a legal or a moral stake in the results. In McClung's books, as in the pioneer narratives of Moodie and Traill, rural women work incessantly, making food, clothing, soap, and furniture; keeping livestock; ploughing, digging potatoes, and taking a hand in harvest time. They bear children without the help of doctors and are up and working the next day. But while Traill celebrates the role of women's labour in creating family prosperity, and looks forward to ease when prosperity is achieved, McClung suggests women's role as domestic and agricultural labourers is often unrecognized and explicitly blames men for women's continued burden of physical toil. Beatings, threats, and criminal indifference are commonplace in the desperate landscape of McClung's stories; exhaustion from overwork and childbearing makes

women passive and self-effacing; the power of a community standard created by men in their own interest, and backed up by the church and the
courts, keeps women silent in the face of physical, emotional, and financial abuse at the hands of their husbands and fathers.

In the story 'Carried Forward' (in the collection *All We like Sheep*),
twelve-year-old Hilda Berry is badly beaten by her father when she tries to
tell him that the housekeeper he has hired is starving his children and
drugging his new baby. Hilda is left alone to care for her family because
her mother has died of 'overwork and childbearing' (*Sheep* 201), and she
is driven to the brink of infanticide trying to cope with child care and
housework, 'work without end, a dizzy round, bewildering and numbing
because there was no end, no hope of achievement' (*Sheep* 208). Her
mother 'never grumbled – never got mad – took it all' (191); and the
mother's final advice to Hilda is to 'learn to speak out ... when you feel
something ought to be said ... Don't let anyone make you so frightened
that you cannot speak' (211). But Hilda finds that speaking out in her
own defence and in defence of her dead mother is not sanctioned by the
community; the group of men who gather at Annie Berry's funeral agree
that her father has behaved perfectly correctly and that the women of his
family are at fault for dying; 'it was quite evident that Luke Berry had
been badly treated' (*Sheep* 186). The minister certifies the community
judgment by remarking that he finds the funerals of young women
unpleasant because 'it is so very difficult for the husband and father'
(200). Only the neighbour women, sitting silently around the casket,
acknowledge that the mother suffered and the daughter will suffer more,
but they are 'afraid to speak' (196); they convert their 'wordlessness' into
energetic house-cleaning. Their sympathy for Hilda remains inarticulate;
their contempt for the 'husband and father' is silent.

For McClung's characters, the word of law, which encodes the standards
of the rural community, literally denies women speech by giving them no
grounds from which to reply to a husband's threats. In *Purple Springs*, Mrs
Paine lives with the threat that her husband will deprive her of her home,
her livelihood, and custody of her children if she defies him. She remains
silent, replying to his threats that 'there [is] nothing for me to say' (*PS*
173). Her husband suspects her silence covers 'something sinister and
unknown' which he must vigorously control; he demands that she speak,
and demands that her speech fit the pattern of expectation he has laid
down. But Mrs Paine's silence is dictated by the word of law, a language
which literally gives her no reply to her husband's threats. The lawyer Peter
Neelands quotes the laws which recognize his right to speak, but deny hers:

'She has no claim on her home, nor on her children. A man can sell or will away his property from his wife. A man can will away his unborn child' (*PS* 185). There is in fact nothing Mrs Paine can say to her husband. Similarly, Annie Gray is silent before the laws which deny her a voice in the custody of her child. As a widow, she has no right to determine the smallest element of her son's life; in the absence of her husband, her father-in-law is automatically the child's legal guardian. When her father-in-law accuses her of having had the child illegitimately, she cannot answer the charge. She remains silent despite severe social ostracism because she knows her silence is her only legal defence: 'Only the unmarried mother has the absolute right to her child' (*PS* 264). She explains to the crusading Pearlie Watson why women cannot speak out to change the laws: 'Women who are caught in the tangle of these laws, as I was, cannot say a word – their lips are dumb. The others won' t say a word for fear of spoiling their matrimonial market' (*PS* 244).

A recurring character in McClung's fiction is the woman who 'masters' language in order to re-signify the category of the feminine: 'the rebellious, the strong-minded, self-determining woman who is not passively acted upon by the society in which she lives' (Hallett and Davis 269). The character of Pearlie Watson (who McClung in her autobiography states is partially based on herself) learns to 'speak out' for herself and for other women in the three books which depict her life: *Sowing Seeds in Danny*, *The Second Chance*, and *Purple Springs*. Remarkable in her childhood for her determination to learn to write and to recite, Pearlie encounters the suffragist movement at the Normal School in Winnipeg and returns home to speak out for her neighbours. She confronts Mrs Paine's husband and the prospective buyer he has found for their farm, and tells Mrs Paine's side of the story: 'I am going to do something for you today that no one has ever done. I am going to tell you something ... Mrs Paine would never tell you' (*PS* 181, 186). She manages to persuade the buyer that the sale should be put off. Pearlie also speaks for Annie Gray by confronting the evil father-in-law with Annie's side of the story, winning his sympathy for her suffering. Finally, Pearlie uses what she has learned about gender and language to confront her lover, Dr Clay, using her position of authority to achieve her goal of marriage to him. Pearlie's ability to achieve linguistic subjectivity, her self-expression, is in itself the source of power which changes society in these stories.

Yet despite the power which the entry into language grants these characters, language is an ambivalent tool in McClung's books because it also limits the ways in which women can be perceived. When Pearlie stands before the Women's Parliament in *Purple Springs*, she does not deliver a speech in favour of women's suffrage: instead, she delivers a parody of the Premier's speech against it. Her act of speaking a man's words in the manner of a specific man, mocking his power and the system of power which gave it to him, literally destroys the Premier, personally and politically. But the words are not hers; rather, Pearlie uses his words, reversed and re-signified by her oppositional position in language.[4] The discourse of political contention does not provide words whereby she can signify herself as public and political, and all she can do is express her 'self' as his opposite.

In none of these stories does the happy ending won by speaking really resolve the issues raised by women's silence earlier in the story; as in the New Woman novels discussed in chapter 4, the 'quest motif' of the story is not resolved by the 'romance ending' (DuPlessis 3–4). Hilda Berry's father remains a brute, with no interest in his children's welfare beyond what the neighbours might think: 'Starved mentally and spiritually they might be, and he would feel no pang of conscience' (*Sheep* 229). Annie Gray is still legally at the mercy of her father-in-law's uncertain temper, despite his recognition of her rights as mother of his grandchild; Mrs Paine has temporarily stalled the sale of her home, but the laws that allow her husband to sell it persist. Pearlie Watson learns how to distance her romantic fantasy of marriage from marriage law through her defence of Mrs Paine and Annie Gray in *Purple Springs*; while she is able in the end to declare her love for Dr Clay, her marriage will still bring her under the confines of the legal contract that victimized her friends. The sentimental happy endings of these stories, in which men miraculously come to a change of heart through the *dea ex machina* of Pearlie's voice, cannot close the issues raised by women's silence and speech, for the entry into language both empowers and subjects.

The story of the Finnish immigrant Helmi Milander in *Painted Fires* dramatizes the ambivalence of language for women. Initially, ability to speak English is represented as a step towards self-actualization for Helmi; it would allow her to escape the life her sister leads in Finland, and protect her from exploitation by men in 'America.' Helmi pursues her dream by immigrating to Canada, where she becomes a domestic servant, signalling her essential moral goodness without language by her obsession with cleanliness.[5] Helmi learns English, but the novel makes it clear that the kind of English Helmi learns is as important as the learning itself: her Christian benefactor, Miss Abbie, tries to reinforce her moral upbringing by teaching her to say, 'Honesty is the best policy' and 'Evil communications corrupt good manners,' while her selfish neighbour, Mrs St John, introduces her to indolence and corruption with 'She has an elegant coat' and 'Have a chocolate? I adore chocolates' (48). The words themselves dictate the choices Helmi faces as she becomes 'Canadianized' – between the position of the criminal female 'foreigner' and that of the good citizen, as defined by Miss Abbie and the English-Canadian community of the novel.

Helmi's silence again becomes an issue when she is arrested in a police raid of a heroin dealer. Her silence represents her moral innocence – she has sworn to protect Mrs St John, who sent her to pick up her supply of the drug – yet her refusal to speak paradoxically both protects and victimizes her. The judge declares, 'If she is innocent, why won't she talk?' (60) and orders her held in custody. At the Girl's Friendly Home, she is especially punished for her refusal to confess, which is figured as stubbornness, pride, and unregenerate evil by the evangelist directors, the Wymuths. During the evening prayer service, Helmi refuses to have her secret 'prayed' out of her (82). She chooses not to enter the discourse of the courts and the Girl's Friendly Home, which would implicitly relegate her to the position of the 'foreigner' on the margins of Canadian society. Instead, she murmurs, 'Skin a mir inka! Skin a mir inka! Skin a mir inka doo! I love you!' (84), defining herself by her identification with the Canadian Girls in Training. Her prayer, which Mrs Wymuth interprets as a strange sort of Finnish piety, perpetrates an ironic joke on the Wymuths and strengthens Helmi in her resolve to keep her secret.

Helmi keeps her secret throughout the novel. Her silence represents her trust in Mrs St John, in her husband, Jack Doran, in God, and in the optimistic promise of eventual success which the CGIT 'Blue and Gold' book holds out to her in sentimental and moralistic verse.[6] Thus Helmi's silence represents her strength and her attempt to dictate the conditions of her own 'Canadianizing.'[7] But another silence, that of Mrs St John, is figured as weakness. Eva St John never officially clears Helmi's name, rationalizing her silence as a duty to protect her husband's reputation. When she finally confesses to her brother, Jack Doran, in the midst of wartime London, she is immediately struck down by flying shrapnel. Her confession of the truth about Helmi's visit to the drug dealer, another form of self-expression, is accompanied by the punishment traditionally meted out to vain women; she is marked for life by a broken nose and a severe facial scar.

The issue of the ways that women can 'express' their authentic selves is vitally linked to linguistic and literary convention in McClung's work. The speaker of McClung's autobiography determines to become articulate, a 'voice for the voiceless,' when she undergoes a crisis/conversion experience during her first pregnancy. She calls for a new kind of language within which to articulate the solidarity she feels with other women who have borne children, and recounts the way that a neighbour's experience of childbearing in poverty can only be articulated publicly as a joke: 'I remembered with particular bitterness hearing the men in our neighbourhood joke about Mrs Jim Barnes who got her husband to move the stairs in their little log house every time another baby was coming. She said it made her feel she had a new house ... I could see Mrs Barnes, a pallid, overworked little Englishwoman, homesick, and old at thirty. They already had more children than their little house could hold. Two little ones had died, but these husky brutes ... could laugh and actually find a cause of merriment in the poor woman's pain' (*Stream* 16–17). McClung's persona vows to find new ways to communicate the 'reality' of women's experience in language, by breaking and re-signifying conventional language. In asserting a desire to represent this reality, McClung's novels assume conventional language, as well as the popular genre of 'domestic family fiction,'[8] as artificial limitations to be broken and discarded in the service of asserting the real. In a narrative strategy common to predecessors like Henry James and Sara Jeannette Duncan, McClung's fiction signifies reality as difference by evoking the conventions of a traditional genre in order to subvert and undermine them.[9]

McClung's stories repeatedly evoke conventional representations of the feminine in order to reveal them as artificial and to substitute new ways of signifying the real.[10] 'It is not a woman's place to work outside like this, don' t you know' (131), protests the English farming student Arthur Wemyss when he sees Pearlie milking in *Sowing Seeds in Danny*. In contrast, female characters like Pearlie, Annie Gray in *Purple Springs*, Helmi Milander in *Painted Fires*, and 'The Bride' in 'The Neutral Fuse' emphasize their capacity and willingness to work inside or outside the home, both for their families and for the community at large. Representations of romantic love are ridiculed repeatedly, as even children can see the contrast between real love and the 'Edythe and Egbert' subplot of *Sowing Seeds in Danny*, or the *Family Herald* stories of *Clearing in the West*. The conventions of the pastoral are contrasted with 'real' rural life in *Clearing in the West* when young Nellie McClung reads Milton: 'there were times when I wondered how happy the mower and the milkmaid and the plowman really were, interesting and romantic as they were to the poet, when he ... knew he was going home to a warm fire and an easy chair ... What did he know about them anyway? Quite likely the milkmaid had chapped hands ... And all of them were probably underpaid and overworked' (*Clearing* 226). The inadequacy of literary and social convention to signify the real in McClung's fiction can result in parody, as in the following generic exhortation, written by McClung's autobiographical persona to express her frustration at being expected to crochet while the boys are studying academic subjects:

> The heights by great men reached and kept
> Were not attained by sudden flight,
> But they, while their companions slept,
> Were toiling upward in the night.
> They did not leave their reading books
> To fool around with crochet hooks;
> They did not slight their history-notes
> To make lace for their petticoats;
> But step by step they did advance,
> And gave no thought to coat or pants!
> So let my steps be ever led
> Away from wool, and crochet thread;
> And let my heart be set to find
> The higher treasures of the mind. (*Clearing* 137–8)

The violent contrast between the expectations raised by the conventional first few lines and the sudden introduction of schoolgirl English ('fool around') and unconventional subject matter (wool and crochet hooks) does more than demonstrate 'Nellie's' literary influence upon that justly famous Prairie poet Sarah Binks; it shows forcefully how the genre of poems which exhort children to hard work and excellence simply do not include 'real' women.

The real in McClung's fiction is signified by two broadly defined cultural codes: the unacknowledged material and emotional hardships of women's domestic lives, and the ways that these hardships either enable or impinge upon the self. 'Reality' is defined as material objects; dirt, ugliness, poverty, and moral weakness are the privileged signifiers of truth. 'Unreal writing does no good, and although I am not fond of sordid ugliness, I prefer being dragged through the sewers of reality, to reading something unrelated to life' (cited in Hallett and Davis 252). McClung specifically rejects techniques associated with modernist realism, and defends the intrusion of authorial moral judgments and the happy ending as important literary techniques. Rejecting the comments of readers who found her work too partisan to be realist, and objected that 'the black [was] too sombre and the white too dazzling' (cited in Hallett and Davis 232) in her characters, McClung champions fiction with a defined social purpose: to represent the lives of women and men as burdened by hard work, temptation, and emotional self-sacrifice, tempered by a 'gleam of hope' that 'must shine through the darkness some place' (cited in Hallett and Davis 245).

The stories justify any departures from conventional narrative resolutions by an appeal to this particular reality, producing 'the real' as, by implication, identical to the representational. In 'Men and Money,' the conventional happy ending does not appear, and the couple who sacrificed personal prosperity to raise two healthy children lose both their sons in the First World War. 'If this were a story – a piece of fiction – a romance – I would give it a different ending. But it is not my story, and I have no option' (*Sheep* 59), explains the narrator. Similarly, 'The Neutral Fuse' disregards conventions of narrative resolution by offering two endings to the story of a woman who is caught shoplifting. In the first ending, the protagonist is summarily convicted and sentenced by a male judge critical of 'club women' ; the story parenthetically explains, '(Now, by all the rules of short story writing, this is the place to end the story, and this is the logical ending. In many cities this would have been the ending, but it so happened in the city of which I am writing that the ending was on this wise)' (*Sheep* 120). The first conclusion, signified as real by the insensitivity of the male judge, is superseded by a real account of the understanding and medical treatment the same woman receives from a female judge and a female psychologist, based on McClung's knowledge of the courtroom practices of her friend Emily Murphy, the first woman police magistrate in the Commonwealth.

That these stories (and the autobiography) use the genres determined by patriarchy to 'voice the voiceless' feminine is perhaps their limitation as feminist advocacy; to assert a difference is always to assert a difference from, and so a relation to. The new 'real' feminine as signified in McClung's fiction has its roots in the very stereotypes it seeks to overthrow. The inner feminine virtues of self-sacrifice and self-control, expressed as the practices of nurturing domestic labour, reproduction and support of the self-made man, mother love, and moral authority are naturalized in McClung's fiction and her essays as constituting the self-expression of a universal feminine woman. In fact, much of McClung's writing is dedicated to producing the 'natural' sphere of women, and statements about women's instinctive 'nature' and characteristic practices are ubiquitous.

'The instinct to house-clean is inherent in women' (*Sheep* 137); 'Women give life, protect life, sustain life, but are "out of character" when they take life' (*Leaves* 110); 'Women are naturally the guardians of the race, and every normal woman desires children' (*In Times* 22); 'The woman's outlook on life is to save, to care for, to help' (*In Times* 23). These works inconsistently evoke both scientific and domestic discourses, as in 'The Neutral Fuse' when a psychoanalyst deduces the characteristics of a woman's mental illness from her understanding of domestic life; to some extent, these texts reassert the primacy of the domestic feminine over science in a kind of backlash against the implications of New Woman fiction. McClung's fiction recalls the work of Catharine Parr Traill and Susanna Moodie in justifying the new feminine practice of labour in the public sphere by appeal to the feminine virtue supposedly located beneath the surface of the material body. McClung's texts in effect produce the feminine woman as a social activist by exhorting her to action based upon her essential nature as mother: 'All this protective love, this instinctive mother love, must be organised in some way, and made effective. There [is] enough of it in the world to do away with all the evils which war upon childhood, undernourishment, slum conditions, child labour, drunkenness. Women could abolish these if they wanted to' (*Stream* 27). That 'organised love' justifies the practice of articulating the reality of the self, and by this means persuading men to change their actions. As Pearlie Watson sees it, men do 'not know just how things stand' (*PS* 179) and need to be told by women: 'Women learned to cook, so that their children might be fed; they learned to sew that their children might be clothed, and women are learning to think so that their children may be guided' (*In Times* 23).

Clearing in the West and *The Stream Runs Fast*, McClung's two volumes of explicit autobiography, provide a demonstration of the way that McClung's writing roots the practice of self-expression in the inner virtues of the domestic woman. The autobiography creates 'Nellie,' the narrated self, as fundamentally responsive to the needs of those around her rather than to her own desire; her self is fundamentally different from that of the traditional male subject of autobiography. The pre-eminent challenge of a woman's autobiography, according to Sidonie Smith in *A Poetics of Women's Autobiography*, is the challenge to a male subject; the writing of an autobiography by a woman is a fundamental challenge to the genre, which is founded on the silence of women. Autobiography, to the extent that it creates and celebrates a separate, autonomous, continuous self, is an exercise in the repression of the mother's voice, and so is fundamentally an assertion of masculine selfhood, 'an assertion of arrival and embeddedness in the phallic order' (40). The creation of the feminine self as self-effacing, defined by relationship and by duty to others, demonstrates the contradiction inherent in the political project of self-expression which McClung promoted for women.

Most critical definitions of autobiography focus, not on the structure of the narrative, but on the self created by the narrative: a unique, essential, autonomous self created by its 'willingness to challenge cultural expectations and to pursue uniqueness at the price of social ostracism' (Smith 9). This 'conventional' autobiographical self rarely appears in autobiography by women (Mason 231, Stanton 14, 16) and indeed does not appear in McClung's autobiography. Instead, the autobiography creates a self identified with domestic ideology, self-effacing, conservative, bound by duty to family and a moral community. Because the woman autobiographer is always read as a woman first, reproduction of the conventional focus on self in a woman's autobiography may be read as self-ish, aggressive, self-aggrandizing (Smith 49); McClung's autobiography deflects attention away from herself and towards her family, her colleagues, and her domestic life.

Part of the autobiography's strategy of self-effacement is the creation of a multiple self, a self who has no self, but is merely the sum of the influence of her family, her experiences with other women, and her choice to be a writer. The account of Nellie's childhood suggests the members of her family 'create' her. She has no characteristics of her own but gets her self-confidence and love of fun from her Irish father, and her personal strength and moral rage for reform from her Scots mother. Her father explains: '[Your mother is] Scotch ... they're very serious people, a little bit stern, but the greatest people in the world for courage and backbone. The Irish are different; not so steadfast or reliable, but very pleasant. Irish people have had so much trouble, they've had to sing and dance, and laugh and fight, to keep their hearts from breaking' (*Clearing* 36). Throughout both volumes of the autobiography, Nellie repeatedly calls on her 'Scotch caution' or her 'Irish temper' to explain her actions; the little girl who likes to dance in front of crowds, but lies awake nights worrying about whether she closed the hen-house door, thus comes to her career as a social reformer and public speaker by heredity.

In addition to becoming the repository of her parents' traits, Nellie becomes the sum of other women's experiences. Her mother, Mrs Mooney, typifies the pioneer woman[11] in the autobiography: 'calm, cheerful, self-reliant, and undaunted' (*Clearing* 82). Strong-willed and courageous, Nellie's mother is also in her own way an artist, providing the civilizing necessities of home-made carpet, curtains, bread, soap, and clothes for her family, and expressing her own creativity in her weaving and sewing. She provides a strong thread of historical continuity in Nellie's feminism.[12] Another model of strength is the 'minister's wife,' a suffrage supporter and member of the WCTU who also delivers babies and teaches Sunday school, creating a 'fine frenzy of high endeavour' (*Stream* 288) in the youthful Nellie, who resolves to be just like her. Negative models of a woman's life also shape Nellie's self. One 'painted doll' sets out to walk from Winnipeg across the prairie in a silk dress and high heels; one farm wife refuses to demand a rearrangement of her farm to make her own heavy burden of work easier. Such women also form Nellie, by providing examples of 'how not to be' and contributing their voices to Nellie's political agitations for more opportunities and better legal protection for women.

But Nellie has few models to show her the way to her chosen career as a writer. She can find only one way for a Prairie girl to become a woman writer; she must become a teacher. Even so, she laments to another aspiring teacher, her friend Bob Naismith: 'Your life is cut out for you Bob, it lies straight ahead, but mine isn't' (*Clearing* 234). Yet even in the choice of a vocation, which is an assertion of self, Nellie is self-effacing. She says her desire to write grows from her feminine altruism; she wants to speak out for the poor and oppressed, and to lighten the burdens of those who toil. She believes that Dickens spoke out for the poor of England, and she hopes, like him, 'to be a voice for the voiceless as he had been a defender of the weak, a flaming fire that would consume the dross that encrusts human souls, and a spring of sweet water beating up through all this bitter world to refresh and nourish souls that were ready to faint' (*Clearing* 281–2). She finds her vocation in the self-abnegation of speaking, not with her own voice, but only with the voices of others; writing becomes duty, and self-expression a moral imperative, for it leads to the righting of wrongs and the defence of the helpless.

Nellie grows up within the strict moral system that her mother determines, and the form of her political life grows out of her mother's response to the conditions of Western life, rather than from a rebellion against it. 'For women ... rebellious pursuit is potentially catastrophic. To call attention to her distinctiveness is to become "unfeminine,"' Sidonie Smith writes (9–10), and, accordingly, McClung's persona is conservative and devoted to her parents. Nellie admires her mother's resourcefulness; this convinces her of women's strength. She experiences her mother's fear of pioneer isolation; this convinces her of the necessity of social programs in rural areas. She laments, with her mother, the loss of her loom; this convinces her of the necessity of women's fight for recognition of their work. Nellie's political concerns are thus presented as an outgrowth of the domestic life of her mother, rather than as a liberal individualist rebellion against it.

Clearing in the West also emphasizes Nellie's closeness to her parents and her conservative mother in order to counter the charge that her feminism arises from permissive, unconventional, or neglectful parenting. Nellie represents a model of mature sympathy with her parents' hard struggle: 'People who write about their own family usually tell much of family tyranny and misunderstanding ... but I have not much to say about parental oppression. My parents were hard-working folk, greatly concerned with the problems of making a living, tired many a time with the day's work and perplexed with life's cares, but they were never too tired or busy to comfort a sad little heart' (Clearing 25). The narrative argues that Nellie's feminism did not arise from rebellion or mistreatment; Nellie does not disagree fundamentally with the generation that came before. Instead, like little Hilda Berry, the heroine of 'Carried Forward,' Nellie carries the debt owed to her mother's generation into the twentieth century.

McClung's statement of her purpose in writing an autobiography makes clear that she is aware of the convention of claiming a personal contribution to history as a justification for autobiography. The introduction to The Stream Runs Fast states that the book will leave a 'legacy of truth' to future generations. 'In Canada we are developing a pattern of life and I know something about one block of that pattern. I know it for I helped to make it, and I can say that now without any pretense of modesty, or danger of arrogance, for I know that we who make the patterns are not important, but the pattern is' (Stream x). The book complains that history books leave out women, giving added force to its claim to document history. But the metaphor of a quilt pattern, which is created by an anonymous woman in her desire to serve her family, reveals an ambivalence about the focus on a single contribution to public life which the genre of autobiography seems to demand. The metaphor diverts attention away from McClung's own role while apparently justifying its importance.

Clearing in the West and The Stream Runs Fast repeat the pattern of diverting attention away from Nellie's personal contribution to history. The account of her contribution to the Women's Parliament, surely her most public success in the Manitoba suffrage fight, refers the reader to the fictionalized Women's Parliament in Purple Springs, and then reprints two newspaper accounts of the evening. Chapters on the suffrage agitation are not chronological narratives of a struggle which proceeded by well-thought-out stages, but collections of witty anecdotes about McClung's speaking engagements and those of her allies. Her participation in the famous 'Person's case' is recounted in fewer pages than her trip to Mexico in old age. Even her birth, arguably an occasion of historical importance in itself, is related in the third person from the point of view of her brother Will, who is disappointed that the new baby is only a girl (*Clearing* 5).

The central episode in Nellie's public career is her 'conversion' to a life of political activism on behalf of other women. In a traditional autobiography, the 'conversion' scene is a moment of revelation which confirms that the uniqueness felt by the protagonist is an asset which will aid in the achievement of a goal. But Nellie's 'conversion' to a life of activism on behalf of women comes, not when she recognizes her uniqueness, but when she becomes pregnant and suffers horribly from nausea: 'my stomach was sick, and I saw no beauty anywhere ... If it had been a man's disease, it would have been made the subject of scientific research and relieved long ago. But women could suffer; it kept them humble! I had heard about the curse of Eve and here it was in full measure. But what useful purpose did it serve?' (*Stream* 15–16). Nellie's miserable physical state leads her to sympathize with the other women she knows who suffer in having children, and to recall the callous treatment of such women by local men. She decides that 'women had endured too much and said nothing,' and pledges that 'women should change conditions, not merely endure them' (*Stream* 16). The contribution to history, which she says is the justification of her book, is thus an act of solidarity with others, of self-effacement in recognition of her common lot with other women. Significantly, Nellie experiences her moment of 'conversion' when she recognizes her kinship with all women, and *not* when she meets a militant suffragette. An earlier episode in which she is taken under the wing of a suffrage supporter and attends a meeting with her prompts Nellie to the resolution that she will never become a political activist (*Clearing* 310). Nellie's experience thoroughly roots her activism in the 'natural' sphere of women, namely, motherhood and children.

Consistent with the surviving fragment of domestic ideology, the auto-biography effaces McClung's sexual life. McClung studiously represses even the expressions of female sexuality which she allows to her characters: the pleasure of breastfeeding, for example, which Helmi Milander enjoys in *Painted Fires*, or the physical attraction felt by the protagonists of 'Red and White.' Nellie's account of hers and Wes McClung's romance and marriage is a cipher, containing few personalized details and no sexual attraction. As a child, Nellie dreams of kisses, ball gowns, lords, emotional crises, and adulterous love affairs, spurred on by the novels and sentimental stories she reads. In contrast, the story of her own courtship and marriage is private and matter-of-fact. Nellie sets out to meet Wes McClung, the son of the local minister, when he is working at the local drugstore; she wants to find out if she can make the minister's wife her mother-in-law. She mentions him once as accompanying her on weekend drives; the next time he appears in the book, she is introducing him to her parents as her future husband. No first kiss, no other potential loves, no crisis over choice of husband appear in the book; instead of expressing the sexual desire of a woman, the book enacts the self-control and modesty of the domestic woman in order to refocus the story of a woman's life beyond marriage.

The effacement of self in *Clearing in the West* and *The Stream Runs Fast* creates a focus on feminine practice rather than on an individualized inner life. McClung was conscious of this unconventional focus on relationships outside herself and in *Stream* even prints an excerpt from a letter from Laura Goodman Salverson which complains about the external focus. 'If I seem to the reader too introspective and disposed to spend too much time analysing my own feelings and reactions, let my good friend Laura Goodman Salverson take the responsibility ... [She said] I was too objective, too concerned with events, conditions, and developments. Autobiography should have in it the mind and soul of the writer. "Be more personal in your new book," she said' (145). But McClung cannot be 'more personal': while she justifies her political and literary career as an 'expression of self,' she defines that self as non-self, enacting the contradictions of maternal feminist ideology. To dwell on the personal would be to deny that the basis of her writing is to do her duty and to serve others; it would imply that writing was a self-ish, rather than self-less, act. Thus the autobiographies create a self whose constant focus on the needs of others makes her inner life a blank.

Despite the self-consciously literary nature of the autobiography, McClung presents it as an account of actual events, a 'legacy of truth' (*Stream* xiii) to future generations eager to understand how the battle for the vote was won and why the battle for prohibition was lost. Her concept of 'truth,' like the idea of 'reality' which justifies her fiction, is drawn from the dregs of nineteenth-century idealism, and depends upon a popularly articulated progressive cosmology which represents 'truth' as only partially available to a fallen humanity, and in need of constant revision as human understanding becomes more adequate to its demands. The 'truth' and the 'real' are not self-evident, or fiction would be unnecessary. Thus McClung's 'self,' her public career as writer and activist, is subordinated to her 'self-expression,' conceived as her duty to enlighten and guide others through literature. Yet McClung's representations of her crusading political activism also acknowledge the ambivalence of her project to articulate the 'reality' of women; language itself is a limitation to representation of the real, and while McClung's work consistently challenges and breaks the stereotypical representations of femininity which she inherited, it does so in the name of a self constructed by the virtues of domestic femininity.

6

Femininity and the Real in
As for Me and My House

As for Me and My House cites the domestic ideal of earlier fiction in order
to undermine its validity. In creating a feminine character who would
appear real to a modern reading audience, *As for Me and My House* draws
upon the psychoanalytic model of human personality to create a character of 'surface' and 'inner depth,' whose unconscious motives and desires
are constitutive of her femininity. Domesticity thus appears as the deceptive surface; the Freudian narrative of the 'masculinity complex' appears
as the gendered inner self which motivates feminine practice in the
novel. The unresolved tension between two discourses of femininity, the
domestic and the psychological, is exacerbated by the 'interrogative'
mode of the text, which lacks an interpretive meta-discourse which fixes
meaning. Together these create the reading practice which is commonly
applied to this text: the search for stable meaning, which is at once the
truth of the text and the truth of Mrs Bentley as a woman.

As for Me and My House takes the form of the private diary of Mrs Bentley, the wife of a minister in the small Prairie town of Horizon; because
the novel consists of nothing but her diary entries, she is the only authority on what happens. As John Moss points out, 'all that we receive as readers is the product of Mrs Bentley's mind ... reality and consciousness
share mutual boundaries' (139–40). Mrs Bentley does not merely report
incidents; she interprets and comments upon the action, and her comments are the sole authority on their meanings. A characteristic diary
entry, in fact, is mainly Mrs Bentley's interpretation of events, containing
little in the way of direct reportage and little verbatim dialogue. Philip
Bentley himself, who is the focus of Mrs Bentley's narration, speaks (in
quotation marks) only twice in the first fifty pages of the novel. His personality, as well as that of all other characters in the text, is composed
(mainly) of interpretations by his wife.

Thus the question of Mrs Bentley's authority to determine truth as narrator is central for readers and critics of *As for Me and My House*. Conventionally, private texts offer the self of the narrator as a guarantee of truth; the intimate knowledge of the narrator gained by the reader's privileged access to her private self creates the illusion of complete revelation, and thus of complete truth.[1] However, Mrs Bentley's own admission of her misinterpretation (or concealment) of her relationship with Paul opens up the possibility of other misinterpretations or concealments. Such misinterpretations mark her as an example of the modernist convention of the unreliable narrator, an unintegrated or neurotic character whose unconscious motives and repressed feelings drive the text away from 'fact' towards self-justification or fantasy. The reader's task then becomes the winnowing of fact from the narrative, and applying the fact backwards to create a new perspective upon the character of the narrator. In this sense, *As for Me and My House* is an example of what Catherine Belsey calls 'the interrogative text,' the text which, because it lacks 'a single privileged discourse which contains and places all the others,' seems to invite the reader to supply 'an answer or answers to the questions it poses' (92). *As for Me and My House* evokes this reading technique in order to produce Mrs Bentley as a very specific kind of personality, a creature with a complex inner life comprised of both conscious and unconscious motives, self-justifications, and angers.

The metaphor of the 'false front' thematizes this creation of psychological depth in the novel. The false fronts of the buildings in the small town of Horizon are evoked by the text as metaphors for the self, constructing personality as consisting of a surface appearance which conceals depth. Offering this metaphor as an appropriate characterization of the self, the text explicitly invites the reader to see Mrs Bentley as a construct of 'surface' and 'depth' as well: her performance of the role of the 'parson's wife' is given as a surface which conceals her true self from Horizon. Mrs Bentley thus characterizes herself as a hypocrite and similarly accuses her husband of hiding an authentic self beneath a deceptive surface. These metaphors reify personality as a construct of surface appearance and inner depth, and invite readers to consider the text itself as a surface which conceals the real Mrs Bentley, her psyche or unconscious self. This real Mrs Bentley is created by reading in the gap between two incompatible textual 'surfaces': the code of the domestic woman and that of gendered psychological subject.

Mrs Bentley claims the authority to produce and interpret her husband's personality on the basis of her conformity to the domestic ideal, which holds that the wife intuitively knows her husband's emotional states and is authoritative on his desires and motivations. While submerging or negating her sense of self as a separate person, the true domestic wife and mother functions to produce and to recognize the essential selves of the members of her family; her intuitive ability to divine the true nature of the desires and fears of her family members enables her to guide their actions in the ways of self-control and self-fulfilment. Mrs Bentley claims the authority to interpret her husband's actions and emotional states on the basis of her intimate knowledge of him as his wife: 'We've lived so long together that we sense and know such things' (49). Thus her very femininity, and its natural truth, becomes a guarantee of the truth of her statements about Philip. On the grounds of her nature as a woman and her position as a wife, Mrs Bentley claims the authority to interpret her husband's actions as expressions of his desire to leave the church, his shame at his own hypocrisy, and his sense of personal failure. She also claims the right to recognize his true essence as an artist and to articulate his needs in the expression of that essence, whether they be domestic support, new paints, or extramarital affairs. Like a wife from a sentimental Victorian novel, she claims the natural ability to know these things without being told, divining them by an intuitive knowledge of her husband's nature which is her defining characteristic as a woman.

Mrs Bentley's role in the marriage is that of the home-maker 'acting out a "nesting" instinct that Penelope would admire' (Kroetsch, 'Afterword' 218), choosing food and cooking meals, arranging furniture, planning and making purchases of clothing, entertaining guests, cleaning.[2] She unhesitatingly sacrifices her own material comfort to her husband's life and his career; after all, he's the one with the study, the books, and the paints. She plans meals to please him, she thinks of his comfort when she practises piano, she is sexually faithful, she supports his work with hers in the Ladies Aid and with the choir. More significantly, she admits to submerging her own ambitions in her role as wife and lover to her husband: 'Submitting to him that way, yielding my identity – it seemed what life was intended for' (22). In doing so, she has become 'a failure ... a small-town preacher's wife instead of what I so faithfully set out to be' (23). But she does not live with a sense of her failure; rather, she 'ha[s] to stop deliberately like this to remember' (23) that she did not fulfil her ambition to be a concert pianist. She believes that her marriage and her husband's love are worth what she gave up: 'To have him notice, speak to me as if I really mattered in his life, that's all I want or need. It arranges my world for me, strengthens and quickens it, makes it immune to all other worlds' (23).

Mrs Bentley's attitude to art also labels her a domestic woman. Her own artistic preferences are Romantic (she loves Liszt and finds Bach dry), and her theory of the nature of the artist is clearly romantic as well;[3] but her ideas about Philip's work are also feminine, personal rather than objective, and rooted in an emotional response to the familiar. Philip suggests she overestimates the value of his work because of her emotional response: 'These things all mean something to you because you've lived in these little Main Streets – with me while I was doing them. You're looking at them, but you're not really seeing them. You're only remembering something that happened to you there. But in art, memories and associations don't count. A good way to test a picture is to turn it upside down. That knocks all the sentiment out of it, leaves you with just the design and form' (202). While Philip's comments show his inclination towards the modernist idea of 'autonomous form,'[4] Mrs Bentley goes into 'dithyrambs about humanity in microcosm' (106), and this articulated, expressed emotion is what labels her response as feminine throughout the book. In contrast, men in the novel participate in the masculine code of 'cool,' resisting the impulse to express emotion and making themselves understood, according to Philip, 'without splurging all over the place about it' (138).

Reviewers of the novel on its initial publication clearly found Mrs Bentley's credibility as narrator solidly founded in her citation of the domestic ideal. Roy Daniells was not the only reader who judged Mrs Bentley 'pure gold and wholly credible' (37) on the grounds of her sympathetic and loving portrait of her husband; G.B., writing in the *Winnipeg Free Press*, found Mrs Bentley so feminine as to constitute an extraordinary, rather than a typical, woman: 'Mrs. Bentley's understanding of Philip's situation, her devotion to him in the face of continual negligence is admirable ... she lives when the book is laid aside. But she lives as an ideal, rather than as a reality' (15–16). William Deacon judged Mrs Bentley to be a 'normal good woman' rather than the embodiment of an ideal, but his comments on her relationship with Philip real-ize the domestic ideal: 'The radiance of her courage and steadfast love, if a feeble light, is convincingly true' (19).

This stereotype of domestic femininity is predicated upon a separation of work and domestic life, in which work is located outside the home and implicitly threatens a man's sense of self, his tender emotions, and his moral integrity, and domestic life is a haven and refuge from the outside world. Interpreted within this discourse, many aspects of Mrs Bentley's relationship with her husband become part of that refuge from the prying eyes associated with his work. Alone together in their home, Mrs Bentley and her husband share intimate knowledge of Philip's essential

self:[5] his painting, his views on the Old Testament, his memories of childhood, his (supposed) desire for Judith, and his personal identification
with Steve. The sheltering of his supposed unbelief, his hypocrisy as Mrs
Bentley calls it, under the domestic roof makes Philip almost paradigmatic of the nineteenth-century concept of alienation of labour, whereby
the worker is forced to sell his labour but has no intrinsic emotional identification with the product created. According to this model, domestic
felicity in the form of rest, physical ease, and emotional acceptance, combined with the woman's role as a man's conscience or moral guide,
restore him to his best self.

Mrs Bird and her husband repeat the domestic ideal in preserving the
separation between public and private life in their marriage, while Mrs
Finley destroys it by importing her public self into her household. Mrs
Bird is clearly eccentric by the town's standards; she dresses in twelve-
year-old tweeds ('Good to begin with') when she goes to call and eats
cookies from a package, a damning statement on her skills as a housewife.
Yet her conversation shows how perfectly preserved the traditional gender differences are in her marriage. She regrets that in Horizon the life
of the mind is limited to men, yet she finds her husband's world alienat-
ing to her emotional life, too 'cold, scientific' (29); she performs the
domestic role within it by adding the 'human touch' (114) to his articles.
Most importantly, she preserves their harmonious marriage by preserving
a complete separation between their public and private lives: 'We serve
the town, but we don't submit to it. Our private lives are our own' (29).
Her opposite is Mrs Finley, who governs her private life and that of her
husband utterly by the repressive standards of the town – in fact, she is
the public guardian of those standards. She clearly expects her reputation as a 'good wife and mother' to excuse her violence in the service of
town morality when she strikes Steve and, later, Philip. Mrs Bird expresses
contempt for Mrs Finley's claims to superior morality, but she does so in a
way that naturalizes the domestic ideal rather than rejects it. Mrs Bird
complains: '"Such a good woman," people keep on saying [of Mrs Finley]
like so many sheep, "such a good wife and mother!" You'd think the rest
of us ran bawdy houses, or fed our husbands powdered glass' (80). Mrs
Finley's claims to authority based on her status as a 'good wife and
mother' are worth nothing, says Mrs Bird, because they are predicated on
the assumption that 'the rest of us' are not good wives and mothers, an
assumption which is false. Mrs Bird's rejection of Mrs Finley produces the
majority of ordinary women as, primarily, good wives and mothers.

The pipe Mrs Bentley finds hidden in a 'cranny up near the ceiling'

(19–20) of the back porch is central in this narrative of home as refuge. A pipe is a forbidden pleasure in the Protestant sect within which Philip ministers, and when Philip used to smoke he did it 'late at night, when there was no chance of anyone coming to discover him or smell the smoke' (20). Mrs Bentley 'used to fill it for him, light his match, and then draw up a stool,' and her participation made them 'partners in conspiracy' (20) to preserve Philip's essential self in spite of the confinement of his role as minister. The pipe and the need for secrecy about it confirms the separation of work and home and validates Mrs Bentley's role as a comfort and refuge against the outside world. However, Philip comes to violently reject both the pipe and the separation which it represents. He throws the pipe in the fire, saying 'since he couldn't smoke in daylight like a man he wouldn't smoke at all' (20).

In rejecting the pipe, and the replacement Mrs Bentley orders, Philip rejects her authority to know his desire, to know him better than he knows himself, and this rejection is part of a generalized undermining of the authority which Mrs Bentley draws from the discourse of domesticity in this text. While Mrs Bentley asserts the authority of a 'woman's way' (85) in interpreting her husband's actions and his emotional life, the text presents her as unable to correctly interpret his life or her own. She claims that Philip doesn't like to display his paintings, but in fact he does so, on several occasions, and presents Laura with a portrait of her horse; she suggests that Philip is an ineffectual minister when he does bring comfort, especially to the Partridge Hill congregation; she says that he is a hypocrite, though his actions in taking in Steve seem stereotypically Christian; she says that he blames her for his failure as an artist, when, in one of the few direct speeches in the novel, he takes the blame upon himself (157).[6] Mrs Bentley's inadequate knowledge of her husband's essential self indicates a failure of the domestic ideal as a framework for representing feminine psychology, and the evocation of an additional cultural code, that of modern psychology.

The psychological model is evoked by Mrs Bentley's own admissions of her errors in judging both Philip and herself. The novel is riddled with examples of her recasting her ideas about Philip and rejecting her previous judgments about his actions: she changes her idea that he needs a stable domestic life and comes to believe he needs the life of a romantic artist; she speculates about his motives in accusing her of a relationship with Paul; she variously says she has lost his love, or regained it. At the ranch, she admits to being more 'priggish' than her self-presentation has suggested: 'My heresy, perhaps, is less than I sometimes think' (123). She admits to having misrepresented her relationship with Paul: 'All the time I thought it was only Philip, something he was trying to imagine' (207). She admits to trying to manipulate Philip into marrying her, Paul into liking her, Steve into accepting her 'twisted' maternal love. She admits to having 'masculine' elements in her character and to taking on masculine roles. The gaps and incoherencies created by Mrs Bentley's recastings of her judgments, admissions of error, and misinterpretations have the effect of destabilizing meaning in the text, inviting the reader to produce an 'unconscious' of the text which motivates Mrs Bentley to conceal facts and to justify her own actions. Like the Freudian unconscious, composed of repressed drives, needs, and angers, the unconscious produced by the gaps in the text reveals itself to (is created by) the listener/reader 'unwittingly' (Cude 79) in the act of reading, its existence and its composition being produced by the process of interpretation.

The production of the 'unconscious,' and with it the undermining and eventual rejection of the domestic ideal in the construction of feminine fictional characters, might be represented simply as a technical advance towards verisimilitude; as Wilfred Cude argues: 'After all, Mrs Bentley is a very believable human being: and one of the characteristics that render her believable is her tendency to misunderstand events that concern her greatly' (77). Angela Esterhammer also considers the instability of meaning in the novel to be a sign of its accuracy in representing 'us.' She argues that the dreams depicted in *As for Me and My House* and in Ross's other works suggest 'the many ways *we* resist objective reality: by imposing *our* dreams on it, by perceiving only what is significant to *us* in it, by constructing *our* own narratives out of it' (22, my emphasis). From this view, the instability of Mrs Bentley's judgments of herself and her husband, therefore, is merely 'real.' However, the idea of the 'real' is a fiction itself signified by the text: rather than simply undermining all notions of the real, *As for Me and My House* undermines the domestic ideal in order to naturalize by contrast what is offered as its substitute, the unstable, driven, self-deceiving self of psychology.

Psychological theorists such as Havelock Ellis and Freud rejected the simple identification of good women with the domestic ideal of self-sacrifice, maternal love, and sexual purity, creating a new model of the interior lives of both women and men that emphasized the instability of gender and the existence of repressed sexual drives. The main elements of this model are well known: the determining effect of childhood sexual feelings upon adult behaviour, the repression of such feelings into the unconscious, the development of neurosis from such repressed feelings, and the centrality of narrative in the revelation of the unconscious sources of behaviour. *As for Me and My House* functions as a case study in the literature of psychology, inviting readers to interpret its omissions and inconsistencies as evidence of concealments and neuroses, and to mobilize specifically Freudian stereotypes of femininity to attribute Mrs Bentley's unreliability as narrator to the instability of femininity itself. The fact that Ross read Freud, Ellis, and other psychologists while a young man in Saskatchewan, surreptitiously receiving the mail-order books in a plain brown wrapper, suggests that he may have programmatically created Mrs Bentley as an illustration of the 'masculinity complex.'[7] However, the ideas that Freud codified as science were pervasive cultural stereotypes through which he as well as other intellectuals interpreted the psychology of women. There is certainly no doubt that readers of Ross have used Freudian ideas to provide the 'answers' to the questions posed by the (interrogative) text: David Stouck has remarked upon Mrs Bentley's 'power to castrate' (98) her husband in a judgment which Morton Ross terms a 'Freudian misprint' (194). However, the catalogue of accusations against Mrs Bentley's 'personality' cited by Morton Ross – 'she is arrogant, obtuse, stubborn, hypocritical, manipulative, smug, dowdy, petty, deceptive, self-indulgent, jealous, mean, bitchy, self-dramatising, bitter, subject to delusions, fussy, morose' (194) – certainly suggests without naming the Freudian masculinity complex.

The detailed correspondence between the narrative characterization of Mrs Bentley and the Freudian narrative of the Oedipus complex in women suggests just how widespread and well accepted were the cultural ideas within which Freud defined the masculinity complex. Freud argued that women's sexual life 'is regularly divided into two phases, of which the first has a masculine character, while only the second is specifically feminine. Thus in female development there is a process of transition from the one phase to the other' ('Female Sexuality' 228). While Freud locates this transition from masculine activity to feminine passivity in the individual's infancy, *As for Me and My House* locates a directly analogous shift in Mrs Bentley's late adolescence, when her 'masculine attitude to music' (198) shifts to a feminine desire for Philip: 'he came and the piano took second place ... I forgot it all, almost overnight' (22). This desire, for Freud, is a response to the female child's recognition of the 'fact' of her 'castration,' and represents a desire to gain a penis, in the first instance literally, and in the second, in the form of a son given to her by the father. Mrs Bentley's desire for a son is evident throughout the novel, not only in her desire for Philip's biological son but also in her desire to possess Steve, the foster son Philip has chosen.

The direct relationship between Mrs Bentley's abandonment of her 'masculine attitude to music' in her desire for a son is revealed in her likening of her maternal love for Steve to her love of music. In the following passage, her feelings for her stillborn child (born twelve years before) are equated to her feelings for Steve, and both expressed as equivalent to her (now abandoned) ambitions to be a concert pianist: 'I didn't know anything like that could happen to me. It was as if once, twelve years ago, I had heard the beginning of a piece of music, and then a door had closed. But within me, in my mind and blood, the music had kept on, and when at last they opened the door again I was at the right place, had held the rhythm all the way' (91). In her embrace with her foster son, Mrs Bentley feels music performance 'in her mind and blood': the son and the career are created as structurally equivalent, the one compensating for the other. Mrs Bentley's obsession with her dowdy appearance, her intermittent feelings of ugliness and inferiority (14), her sense that she has wasted her husband's youth and destroyed his career (7), as well as her inability to maintain friendships with women (102) and her possessive jealousy of Philip's relationships (15) are other textbook reactions to the 'fact' of her castration.[8]

Mrs Bentley's inability to live out the narrative of feminine selfhood to its conclusion, that is, to the bearing of a son and therefore to the acceptance of her femininity and the stabilizing of her marriage, is a source of neurosis. This neurosis eventuates in a phantom illness, including pains in her arm and shoulder which prevent her from performing housework and require treatment by Dr Bird with sedatives (79). Because she cannot possess the penis/self of the son, she continues to desire the penis/self of her father/husband in a way which is clearly neurotic, and which she herself recognizes as immature and inappropriate. 'All these years I've been trying to possess him, to absorb his life into mine, and not once has he ever yielded ... It's the reason perhaps I still care so much, the way he's never let me possess him, always held himself withdrawn. For love, they say, won't survive possession. After a year or two it changes, cools, emerges from its blindness, at best becomes affection and regard. And mine hasn't' (84–5). Many of the feelings Mrs Bentley expresses towards her husband seem to be inappropriately maternal and therefore expressive of her desire to dominate her husband as if he were a child. This impression is confirmed in the last line of the novel, when Philip asks her if she might not confuse him with their child if she names it Philip as well: 'That's right, Philip. I want it so' (216). For, according to the norms of patriarchal society, the child is the means whereby Mrs Bentley gains power and status; she is now in charge of something tangible belonging to her husband, his biological son and the bearer of his name, though the child is 'all [she has] of him' (207). She has finally got what he has, through her agency as mother. And in the psychological model, the son *is* confused with the father in the narrative of femininity; he is, in some senses, identical to him. For, according to Freud, confusing the son with the father is the *only* way that a woman can achieve unconflicted feminin- ity and a stable marriage: 'A mother is only brought unlimited satisfaction by her relation to a son; this is altogether the most perfect, the most free from ambivalence of all human relationships. A mother can transfer to her son the ambition which she has been obliged to suppress in herself, and she can expect from him the satisfaction of all that has been left over in her of her masculinity complex. *Even a marriage is not made secure until the wife has succeeded in making her husband her child as well and in acting as a mother to him*' ('Femininity' 133–4, my emphasis). Balked in her drive to 'possess' the penis/power of a man through the birth of a son, Mrs Bent- ley has been unable to transfer the energy of her libido to its proper object, and she remains neurotically dependent upon her husband's love.

Yet not just any male child will resolve the issues raised by Mrs Bentley's recognition of her lack. The son must be capable of bestowing the power of patriarchy on the mother by his embodied citation of the norms of patriarchal descent. Steve, while he makes a good temporary stand-in, is ineligible because his father is unknown and, because 'foreign' and Cath- olic, disenfranchised by the society of Horizon. The father of Judith's baby is equally unknown,[9] yet Mrs Bentley's strong belief that he is the child of her husband allows him to function as the partner in that per- fectly unconflicted relationship, and thus to heal her of the neurosis of her femininity.

The attribution of Judith's baby to Philip is thus central in establishing the 'truth' of Mrs Bentley, for through that baby she is offered the oppor- tunity to become maturely feminine, a real woman. Thus *As for Me and My House* evokes the relationship between the paternity of male children (the 'truth' of a woman's body) and the truth of the text which is central to classic realist fiction, for it is upon women's truth that Mrs Bentley's reli- ability as narrator turns. The relationship between paternity and truth is established by Mrs Bentley's narrative of Philip's life. Philip is illegitimate, yet, according to the novel, he knows (certainly?) who his father was. His entire life, according to Mrs Bentley, is an attempt to establish the truth of his lineal descent from this putative father by carrying on with the cre- ated fiction of his life. For his illegitimacy, he blames his mother, and all women:[10] 'towards even [the] memory [of his mother] he remained implacable' (40). Because he was born illegitimate, Philip judges that no

living woman can ever be true, and truthful; the only truthful woman is
Judith, who by dying in childbirth is rendered incapable of deceiving. But
a live woman can always be untrue – if not now, sometime later. She is
always potentially deceptive; her body may be concealing something, just
as Mrs Bentley's text may conceal adultery, anger, masculinity, ambition.
The instability of the text reinforces the potential of all women, by their
nature, to be secret, to conceal, to deceive. The secret of the feminine
body is the secret of the text demonstrating its instability, its uncontrolla-
bility, its hiddenness. Yet the feminine body cannot be forced to give up
its secret; Judith's baby cannot be securely attributed, any more than the
text itself can be stabilized by the delineation of one chain of evidence to
support that attribution. This instability is not a postmodernist rejection
of stable meaning but a reinscription of an old story: it is the instability of
a woman's body, whose secret is never revealed in the realist text, yet
remains the goal of representation.

By challenging the ideology of domesticity and evoking the discourse of
modernist psychology, the novel defines Mrs Bentley as always/already
unstable and hidden. Because of her lack, her deviation from the male
norm (the 'fact' of her castration), she is incapable of being 'normal'; the
proper name 'I' in this text will always signify inferiority, unattractiveness,
dependence, passive-aggressiveness, jealousy, and contempt of other
women. Because she is unable to negotiate the complex narrative of femininity to its conclusion, the achievement of a male child, she has little
hope of outgrowing her sense of competition with men and her grievance
at being born female. In addition, because she is female and holds the
secret of paternity, she is always hidden; the revelation of the hidden,
which is the aim of realist fiction, is always frustrated by her potential
deceptiveness.

The success of Mrs Bentley as a signifier of reality is confirmed by the
chorus of readers who have found the narrator to be 'a very believable
human being' (Cude 77). It is not surprising that we find her realistic, for
she is who we think we are (or thought we were until we read Foucault).
'Mrs Bentley was everything I did not want to be, everything I hated and
feared, but unconsciously felt in danger of becoming with marriage and
especially with the production of children,' writes Helen Buss of her reac-
tion to the novel as a young woman ('Who Are You' 205). The universality
and truth of the psychological model of the feminine self has formed the
basic assumption of criticism of the novel: analysis of Mrs Bentley's narrative for its concealments, fantasies, and self-justifications, as well as the
revelation of the motives for each of these, has until recently been the

mainstream of criticism. Even feminist critics, 'seeking a Mrs Bentley that accords with female experience' ('Who Are You' 191), have failed to identify her as a linguistic construct and have sought to defend her from charges of meanness, hypocrisy, inhumanity, barrenness, and manipulativeness,[11] as though she were a person whose material and historical situation has determined (or excused) her supposed defects of character. Critics have relied so exclusively upon the technique of 'analysing' the inconsistencies, omissions, and errors in Mrs Bentley's narrative as self-revelatory of unconscious, concealed, or suppressed aspects of her personality that Frank Davey has recently reminded us of the obvious, that the narrator of the novel 'is not a free-standing agent whose "personality" can explain the emphases and omissions of the novel, but a textual effect partly constituted by these emphases and omissions' (178).

Considering the role of fiction in the reproduction of the reader as subject, it seems likely that the anxiety of readers to stabilize the personality of Mrs Bentley is in fact an anxiety to stabilize themselves in relation to it. Critics such as W.H. New and Robert Kroetsch have suggested that this is a fruitless task, not merely because the text offers no stable meaning, but because stable meaning itself – and the stable subjects which it reproduces – are no longer the necessary fictions of our lives.[12] However, this seems anachronistic as well as unsatisfying. If Ross is an unconscious precursor of postmodernism, then the 'subject' of the novel (both the 'personality' of Mrs Bentley and the reader who recognizes her) loses its specificity and is in danger of being regarded as natural rather than historical and ideological. The subject of a novel written fifty years ago is not identical to 'us,' and a residue of historical otherness remains unassimilated to the postmodernist reading of the text. Only by leaving this historical otherness unread can the reader construct Mrs Bentley as a paradigmatic artist in conformity with current interpretative orthodoxy; this orthodoxy erases the ideological work the novel performs in transforming the domestic ideal, and its basis of interpretive authority, into neurosis and reinscribing the feminine according to the Oedipal thrust of the classic realist novel as the unknown, deceptive, and mysterious enigma at its heart.

By reproducing Mrs Bentley according to the narrative of modern psychological femininity, *As for Me and My House* dramatizes a rejection of the domestic ideal in modernist writing generally; indeed, for some critics, modernism and misogyny are inseparable. A backlash against feminist successes in the late nineteenth century and early twentieth century suggests modernism itself arose from anxiety about the nature of women and their relations to men: 'the literary phenomenon ordinarily called "mod-

ernism" is itself ... a product of the sexual battle'(Gilbert and Gubar xii).
'To many late nineteenth and early twentieth-century men, women
seemed to be agents of an alien world that evoked anger and anguish'
(4), and their response was the 'fear of emasculation that characterized
so much modernist literature, a fear that was often associated by men of
letters with a moral and spiritual as well as a psychological fall'(43).
The fact that so many male modernist writers used emasculation or the
triumph of a strong female character to express supposedly 'universal'
modernist angst is a reflection of this fear, according to Gilbert and
Gubar: 'though they do, of course, express angst, it is significant that
these modernist formulations of societal breakdown consistently
[employ] imagery of male impotence and female potency' (36). Examples of the use of imagery of emasculation to express modernist despair
include Joyce's *Ulysses* and Faulkner's *Light in August,* two of the texts
cited by Ross as among his favourites.[13]

Thus, with Helen Buss, I find those critics who accept Mrs Bentley as
'real' to be deeply afflicted by the 'fear of women' which Robert Kroetsch
identifies as definitive of masculinity in the novel.[14] The critics mimic the
novel's cowboy sensibility, by simultaneously creating and rejecting Mrs
Bentley through the evocation of cultural codes of the modern psychological subject, whose surface conformity to the code of the domestic
woman is of necessity concealing a threatening other. *As for Me and My
House* undermines the validity of feminine authority by contrasting
domestic ideology with modern analytic psychology, creating in Mrs Bentley the backlash against feminism which characterized the early modern
period. Perhaps this is the reason why it is the only novel unanimously
agreed upon by Canadian scholars as a true classic of the modern period.

Conclusion: Citing and Reciting

We are complicit, yes. Folded into the wreckage of grief and power.

Daphne Marlatt, *Taken*

This book has argued a thesis which may be read, in traditional Canadian style, as both deeply conservative and deeply radical. Through readings of texts by women and men, it has suggested that escape from the hierarchy of gender is not as simple as some feminist criticism of Canadian texts would suggest, for gender is inscribed in the subject as part of its formation; gender, in life as well as in texts, is formative of the self. All of the texts examined here self-consciously take femininity as their subject, and work to naturalize Woman as a category of the individual self whose determining attribute is her gender. In this they 'cite' the gender ideal, creating subjects according to a socially constructed gender norm which links feminine actions, behaviour, 'practice,' to the specific qualities and virtues of a gendered inner self. In the work of Traill, Moodie, and Leprohon, these qualities, such as self-command, self-sacrifice, love of home, and submission to duty and maternality, are derived from the domestic ideal; in New Woman fiction and the work of McClung and Ross, the domestic self is challenged by various scientific discourses of femininity which attribute to women a biological heterosexuality which drives them to bear children (specifically male children) and to participate in human evolutionary development.

The practice of 'citing' the gender ideal arises because the gendered inner self is itself a fiction which can never satisfactorily materialize in a body, no matter how the configuration of that body might be perceived. Gender must be established and re-established in language and in practice, because material appearance does not establish its reality. Thus, in taking Woman as their subject, these texts represent a submissive response to interpellation by bourgeois patriarchal ideology. This response is not silence; rather, these texts grasp the limited authority which feminine subjectivity grants in order to speak. They work to conceal a perceived dichotomy between the gendered inner self of characters (and authors) and potentially transgressive material practice, not by challenging the gender ideal itself, but by refiguring the seemingly transgressive appearance as conformity to the socially sanctioned ideal. By 'citing' this norm, texts by Moodie, Traill, and McClung qualify their authors as viable subjects, despite their transgressive appearances in the public sphere; novels by Leprohon, Wood, Sime, Fytche, and Ross qualify their characters as 'real' and 'natural' by citing a domestic or scientific norm which justifies their characters' seemingly transgressive actions. These texts do not escape or throw off femininity – they do not even significantly challenge it. Their characters, whether autobiographical or simply fictional, do not move 'beyond' femininity to become masculine, androgynous, or simply people, for gender is a condition of the speech that authorizes them as subjects. Rather, they justify any seeming departures from authorized feminine practice by reiterating their submission to the feminine gender ideal.

The gender ideal which is constitutive of the feminine in the pioneer texts and in *Antoinette de Mirecourt* is the domestic ideal, derived from the 'sexual contract' whereby women take their place in the home as embodiments of nurturance, self-control, and self-sacrifice in return for their protection by men in the public sphere of violence and competition. While the domestic ideal proscribed the transgression of women's separate sphere, the virtues which it assigned to women (such as submission to duty, love of home, dedication to family, and submission to the authority of God and husband) are used in *The Female Emigrant's Guide*, *Roughing It in the Bush*, and *Antoinette de Mirecourt* to authorize the unconventional intrusion into the public sphere which emigration, writing, and political commentary seemed to represent. The resignification of Woman as a biological category (which includes sexual desire) in turn-of-the-century and later texts also represents a form of submission to the hierarchy of gender rather than a rebellion against it, for while the discourse of science altered the content of the category of the feminine it did not change the order of power. Two versions of the feminine self, the biological and the domestic, intersect in the fiction of Nellie McClung, which represents the contradictions inherent in the subject of maternal feminism by creating characters who achieve individual 'self-expression' by 'discovering' their inherent domestic virtues; this contradiction is resolved in *As for Me and My House* when the domestic woman is figured as a false exterior which conceals a purportedly real scientific psychology of woman.

The analysis presented in this book demonstrates, albeit in a limited way, that for women chronological change has not been synonymous with progress, nor has the 'sea-change' produced by emigration and the refiguring of the feminine in Canada produced significant progress towards liberation. *The Female Emigrant's Guide* justifies emigration and the performance in Canada by women of some tasks which were gendered masculine in England on the basis of conformity with a universal and unvarying feminine virtue; it proposes no real change in what a Woman is, but subsumes the new things a woman does under the old domestic definition. *Roughing It in the Bush* and other works by Susanna Moodie similarly justify writing itself (including autobiographical writing) by suggesting that both the form and the impulse for creative work derive from the unvarying inner self of the domestic woman. *Antoinette de Mirecourt* utilizes the concept of the 'sexual contract,' which defines and confines political and domestic speech, to translate political relations between England and Quebec into gender relations and place them under the moral authority of the domestic woman. In these texts, the domestic ideal is not simply oppressive in a generalized way; rather, because it purports to create a sphere of authority for women, it enables their entry into public discourse.

Canadian New Woman fiction has often been read as reflecting social progress towards equal rights for women because it represents women as taking paid work and following narratives of self-actualization; however, this analysis has suggested that the necessity to confess and articulate Woman in the context of new social realities is in itself a form of submission to the hierarchy of gender. By reconstructing the motivation for feminine practice as a biological drive towards heterosexual sex and the conception of children, New Woman fiction more securely encloses women within the category of 'Womanhood.' While shreds of the domestic ideal coexist with a concept of women as biological in the fiction and autobiography of Nellie McClung, these two contradictory ideological formations are 'closed' in McClung's work by the fiction of self-actualization for women, who paradoxically achieve independent selfhood through conforming to the domestic ideal. In *As for Me and My House*, domesticity becomes a deceptive cover for the supposed real psychology of woman, in which the motivations of jealousy and envy can only be assuaged by the birth of a son.

These readings seek to illuminate the practice of 'citing' ideal feminin-

ity, whether that ideal be domestic, psychological, or scientific. This practice extends far beyond the nineteenth- and early twentieth-century
Canadian fiction analysed here, for it also structures much feminist political activism in our own day. The common assertions that women are
more nurturing, ecologically aware, and cooperative and less violent, self-
ish, and abstract than men, assertions which motivate much important
work in eco-feminism, the struggle against violence against women, and
the campaign for good day-care, clearly derive from the practice of citing
the gender ideal, a practice which this study has shown is irretrievably
implicated in the maintenance of patriarchy. This book has argued that
women cannot avoid 'citing' such categories; to the extent that subjectivity is created in language, it offers no subject positions outside the current gender hierarchy. As Luce Irigaray has written, 'the feminine occurs
only within models and laws devised by male subjects. Which implies that
there are not really two sexes, but only one. A single practice and representation of the sexual' (cited in de Lauretis 5). This, then, is the very
conservative thesis, one which, with other activist women, I have found
depressing enough – we cannot avoid being implicated in the way things
are, and it's going to be very difficult to change.

Conversely, this book might be construed as arguing a very radical thesis, which might be summarized as, If we're going to change things, we
have to change everything. In this, this study reiterates the view expressed
by many feminist thinkers that change cannot be limited to the attainment
of equal rights, and that feminist criticism of texts cannot legitimately confine itself to an examination of how those rights are progressively attained.
The notion that society as it stands strives to embody democratic individualism and therefore requires only enough tinkering to extend the notion
of the democratic citizen may be common in the popular press, but its limits are clearly visible, and this study has striven to make those limits clear.
The readings offered in this book oppose the view that feminism can be
merely a lobby group for equal rights, and suggest instead that it must be
a form of critique which questions the whole structure of social meanings,
including the category of Woman and the values of consumerism and glo-
bal capital. Even if, in a form of economic revolution, we could move
beyond hierarchy in our material lives, the traces of dominance and subordination will surely linger in language to structure the ways we view
relationship. Truly, we need to 'think globally,' about language, about
meaning, and about gender even as we 'act locally' on the particular issues
of our workplaces and communities.

Notes

Introduction

1 See *Mary Pratt, passim,* for discussions of how each painting grew from moments in an ordinary day.

2 See *Survival,* 50–1; also Afterword, *The Journals of Susanna Moodie,* 62.

3 See Atwood, Fowler, Thompson, Buss, MacMillan, McMullen and Waterston, and Dean in the Works Cited section.

4 See 'I Looked for It, and There It Was – Gone: History in Postmodern Criticism,' *Essays on Canadian Writing (ECW)* 56 (Fall 1995), 37–50.

5 '(it's a kerchief, we said – we wore them to school with the others practising femininity)' (Marlatt, *Ana Historic* 26).

6 Called by Barrett, the 'Cartesian subject' (86, 90).

7 *Critical Practice,* 73.

8 As it seems to be, for example, in the writing of Helen Buss; see 'Who Are You Mrs. Bentley: Feminist Re-vision and Sinclair Ross's *As for Me and My House.*'

9 I am indebted to John Thurston for the term 'work of words'; his use of the ideas of Frederic Jameson in his analysis of Susanna Moodie has strongly influenced my approach.

10 See Buss, 'Canadian Women's Autobiography,' 154–5, for this interpretation of works by Moodie and Traill.

11 See Belsey, chapters 2 and 3, for an elaboration of the analysis of realism which is compressed here.

12 See Margaret E. Turner, *Imagining Culture,* for an analysis of the way that 'America' was a figure of European imagining.

13 See Antony Easthope, *Literary into Cultural Studies,* 43–61, for an analysis of the concept of literary value as ideological.

14 In arguing against the usefulness of evaluation, I wish to distance myself from

the 'non-evaluative' thematic critics of the 1970s; their work was not premised on the bankruptcy of evaluation as a methodology, but on the initial evaluation that Canadian literature was 'rhetorical' rather than 'imaginative,' and therefore already second-rate. See Northrop Frye, 'Conclusion to *A Literary History of Canada*.'

1: *The Female Emigrant's Guide* as the Mending Basket of Domestic Ideology

1 Bentley does note (in 'Breaking the "Cake"') that women could 'exercise their powers according to the known rules of matrimony,' but this power is restricted, in his view, to 'commanding and receiving the respect of her husband' in the form of a bouquet of flowers (110).

2 Carl Ballstadt points out that Traill's *Backwood* as well as *The Female Emigrant's Guide* 'are the Canadian equivalents of English manuals such as Mrs. John Sandford's *Woman in Her Social and Domestic Character* (1831) or Sarah Ellis's series beginning with *The Women of England* (1839)'; see Ballstadt, 'Introduction,' to the Alcuin Society edition of *The Canadian Settler's Guide*, x–xi, and Ballstadt, 'Catharine Parr Traill,' 156–7.

3 See Thompson, *The Pioneer Woman*, 44.

4 The following account of conduct literature and its relationship to social change is drawn from Nancy Armstrong's *Desire and Domestic Fiction*.

5 That the domestic ideal of feminine behaviour crossed over to the New World is evidenced by Canadian conduct literature which reiterates the stereotype. The narrator of *Letters to a Young Lady on Leaving School and Entering the World* (1855) quotes from Hannah More (French 3) and confines her advice to methods of understanding one's duty, forming one's taste, and regulating one's emotions. Like More, the narrator puts much emphasis on the necessity to efface positive desire and to disguise or deny active emotion: 'angry feelings have frequently small, very small beginnings, and, by being watched, might easily be suppressed – how soon, then, could we conquer this, if indulged in, hydra-headed evil!' (63). An anonymous writer in the Montreal *Instructor* argued that the example of women in becoming 'more domestic, more self-denying, more kind, more contented, and more agreeable' under the influence of religion will persuade others to piety ('Female Influence upon Religion' 35). An article in the *Harp* from 1874 entitled 'Woman's Sphere' asserted: 'Woman's first and only place is her home. Within its sanctuary she will find her mission ... She is destined by Providence to make her home a blissful spot to those around her. It should be full of the merry sunshine of happiness – a cloister wherein one may seek calm and joyful repose from the

busy, heartless world ... her kingdom is not of this world, worldly. The land she governs is a bright oasis in the desert of the world's selfishness' (quoted in Mitchinson, *The Nature* 15). Prose fiction written by British North American women during the period 1820 to 1870 also reiterated the European stereotype, for the majority of the popular fiction written in this period makes only a cursory reference to physical location in North America and gives little room to explorations of differing social customs or economic arrangements; it merely adapted the material circumstances of the New World to resemble the Old as much as possible. In 'Alice Sydenham's First Ball' (1849), by Rosanna Leprohon, the poverty-stricken Alice Sydenham's natural manners and sincerity are contrasted to the artificiality of her rich and fashionable acquaintances. In *Woman As She Should Be* (1861), by Mary E. Herbert of Halifax, Agnes Wiltshire dresses plainly and modestly, and governs her life according to duty, performing charitable works and guiding her family's spiritual and emotional lives. Susanna Moodie's fiction, mainly set in England, is dominated by the theme of the suppression and control of 'passion' in the service of the creation of a prosperous, happy household.

It is difficult to place the concept of the 'English lady' discussed in Elizabeth Thompson's *The Pioneer Woman* (10) in relation to the domestic ideal. Thompson's 'English lady' character type 'belongs to the middle and upper class of English society, and is accustomed to a life of leisure in which she can display her many decorative, drawing-room talents' (10); such a character might be identified with Armstrong's 'aristocratic woman,' who is condemned in most domestic fiction because her main focus is personal display.

6 John Thurston has identified the persistence of a British 'gentlemanly ideal' in the work of Susanna Moodie, which similarly locates masculine virtue in merit, rather than fortune or aristocratic connection, an argument which is consistent with Armstrong. See Thurston, *The Work of Words*, 23, especially note 9.

7 Ballstadt notes that 'in contrast to the English books, Traill's *Guide* is concerned with ... doing for oneself rather than managing others' ('Catharine Parr Traill' 179).

8 Elizabeth Thompson also notes the importance of labour in the creation of a specifically Canadian form of feminine practice; and she notes, without locating, the conviction that femininity is essential and universal: '[Traill] clings to her belief that she is a lady, and that she will always remain a lady, no matter what circumstances might dictate' (40).

9 Letter 34 in the Moodie, Strickland, Vickers family fonds (formerly the Patrick Hamilton Ewing Collection) from Sarah (Strickland) Gwillym to Catherine Vickers, ca 1875. This letter is cited by Mary Lu McDonald in the *National Library News* 19:12 (Dec. 1987), 4.

10 Canadian notices of *The Female Emigrant's Guide* appeared in *Maple Leaf* 4:12 (Dec. 1854), 379–80; in 'The Editor's Shanty,' *Anglo-American Magazine* 6:2 (Feb. 1855), 200–1 and 6:4 (April 1855), 386–9; and in *Irish Canadian* 3:13 (5 April 1865), 5.

11 The *Irish Canadian* review notes that the book's 'addresses to husbands, wives, daughters, servants, as to their relative duties' are among its most useful elements.

12 Marian Fowler (in *ET*) suggests that Thomas Traill's difficulty in adapting to life in Upper Canada (which seems to have resulted in depression) is the source of the absence of male assistance in the *Guide*; Michael Peterman also notes his 'frequent depressions' ('Splendid Anachronism' 180). (Catharine Parr Traill's permissive attitude to alcohol [compared with her sister's temperance] might be noted here.) Whether or not Traill's 'life experience' guided her attitude to male assistance in the text, the resulting male absence is consistent with domestic ideology.

13 The production of homesickness as part of 'female nature' is repeated in Traill's article 'Female Trials in the Bush,' which appeared in 1852, two years before *The Female Emigrant's Guide*: 'It has often been remarked how much more prone to discontent the wives of the emigrants are than their husbands ... woman is by nature and habit more strongly attached to home ... and though a sense of duty will and does operate upon the few to arm them with patience to bear and power to act, the larger proportion of emigrants' wives sink into a state of hopeless apathy ...' (22).

14 'Women's labour in this scheme was critical to capital accumulation. To the extent that women's productive efforts sustained the family in its basic consumption needs, male labour was free to engage in production for exchange on the market (through either commodity production or waged labour); to the extent that the total income from market production need not be expended on consumption, accumulation of capital in the family productive unit could occur' (Cohen, *Women's Work*, 8).

15 As Elizabeth Thompson argues in *The Pioneer Woman*. David Bentley suggests that the qualities here ascribed to the 'inner self' of the feminine woman are those which Traill argues must be acquired by the bush settler in order to achieve 'a close fit between the persevering settlers and their at least partly settled landscape' (Afterword to *Backwoods* 293), allowing the implication to be drawn that their opposites (idleness, artificiality, extravagance) are characteristic of the stereotypical British 'lady' of Thompson's book. However, he recognizes that these characteristics derive from a British model of middle-class virtue when he associates them with Hogarth's series of prints *Industry and Idleness*. The qualities ascribed by Thompson to the British 'lady' are condemned

in British conduct books as part of a generalized condemnation of the lingering stereotype of the aristocratic woman. See Armstrong, *Desire and Domestic Fiction.*

2: The Broken Mirror of Domestic Ideology

1 David Bentley discusses the 'voyage' image in works by Moodie and Traill in 'Breaking the "Cake of Custom."'

2 The account of Rachel Wilde's marriage and her preparation for emigration given in 'Trifles from the Burthen of a Life' (reprinted in *Voyages: Short Narratives of Susanna Moodie,* ed. John Thurston) is repeated in *Flora Lyndsay,* and will be cited from that source.

3 All quotations from *Roughing It in the Bush* are taken from the 1989 edition in the New Canadian Library series, which reprints the complete text of the second edition with additions published by Bentley in 1852.

4 John Thurston argues persuasively that the instability of Moodie's attitude to a literary career in this period of her life arose from her association with evangelical Anglicanism and her later conversion to Congregationalism: in this context, her literary career would appear among the worldly ambitions which would contradict her piety (*Work of Words* 46–52). In addition, he argues that Moodie's view of literary genius as above worldly considerations such as making a living contradicted the necessity she felt to make money by her writing (*Work of Words* 26). This is not inconsistent with my argument, which would place piety among the attributes of the domestic woman and confirm the opposition between writing for amusement and writing as commercial pursuit.

5 See also *Roughing It,* 144–5: 'the rigour of the climate subdued my proud, independent English spirit, and I actually shamed my womanhood, and cried with the cold. Yes, I ought to blush at evincing such unpardonable weakness; but I was foolish and inexperienced, and unaccustomed to the yoke.' In this passage, extraordinary endurance of physical pain is assumed to be part and parcel of womanhood.

6 Bina Freiwald has discussed the representation of homesickness as part of the representation of maternal language in '"the tongue of woman": The Language of the Self in Moodie's *Roughing It in the Bush.*' Freiwald argues that Moodie's exaggerated homesickness is part of her strategy of bearing the word, by depicting herself as an abandoned child and literalizing the metaphor of the Mother Country.

7 See, for example, Thurston, *The Work of Words,* 155–7.

8 The inability of the feminine woman to wield authority responsibly even in respect to her own actions implies the necessity of submission to her husband;

yet both husband and wife are subject to the higher authority of Providence. While *The Female Emigrant's Guide* makes some reference to the importance of Christian belief as a sustaining comfort to the female emigrant, *Flora Lyndsay*, 'Trifles,' *Roughing It*, and much of Moodie's short fiction on the theme of emigration verge on the pietistic in their assertion of the role of God's Providence in the fate of their protagonists and 'the necessity of a perfect and child-like reliance upon the mercies of God – who ... never deserts those who have placed their trust in Him' (*RI* 353). John Thurston argues that this emphasis arises from Moodie's personal struggle to accept her lot in life; her evangelistic conversion to Congregationalism a year before her marriage, and her enduring belief in the effects of supernatural forces on individual lives, may also have been factors. However, the repeated inscription of the theme of Providence may also be viewed as gendered practice, conforming to the domestic ideal which ascribes moral and spiritual qualities to the 'soul' of the domestic woman, and enjoins upon her the role of spiritual and moral instructor and guardian of her family, and of society at large.

9 Professor Klinck calls it an 'apprenticeship novel'; Carl Ballstadt notes the traces of the English sketch form and the influence of Mary Russell Mitford on Susanna Moodie's work; Marian Fowler has revealed elements of the sentimental novel and the Gothic in Susanna Moodie's style, her self-presentation, and her characterization of her neighbours; T.D. MacLulich relates *Roughing It* to *Robinson Crusoe* for their common fictions of cultural contact and their patterns of religious conversion. See Ballstadt, 'Editor's Introduction' (xl–xli) for a summary of critical response to the book.

10 Of *Roughing It in the Bush* and C.P. Traill's *Backwoods of Canada*, Buss (1986) writes: 'the writing personae adopted sometimes have an easy sureness that is too formulated, too conventional for the new experiences they describe. On the other hand, since they do not adopt autobiographical personae, they are able, especially in the case of Moodie, to break through the artificiality in order to tell of the ways in which Canada changes their ideas of themselves' ('Canadian Women's Autobiography' 154).

11 Michael Peterman notes that Traill also accepted the assumption that 'it was for men to think – to be analytical, critical, and professional, to assume and perpetuate authority. It was for women to feel and nurture – to be decorous, familial, and retiring, to accept authority's wisdom and beneficence' ('Splendid Anachronism' 177).

12 That Moodie's account of women's thought process constituted conventional wisdom is confirmed by Wendy Mitchinson's survey of Victorian Canadian thought on feminine psychology. For example, she cites William Carpenter in his 1869 text, *Human Physiology*: 'For there can be no doubt that – putting

aside the exceptional cases which now and then occur – the intellectual powers of Woman are inferior to those of Man. Although her perceptive faculties are more acute, her capability of sustained mental exertion is much less; and though her views are often peculiarly distinguished by clearness and decision, they are generally deficient in that comprehensiveness which is necessary for their stability' (Mitchinson, *The Nature of Their Bodies* 36). British reviewers such as Elizabeth Rigby and Henry Chorley agreed that the nature of women's minds made them able observers of the 'close and lively details' of life; the best of women's writings consist of 'miniature touches of life and descriptions of scenes overlooked by the Man in his wide range of view, and often, as to finish, not within the grasp of his more powerful but coarser hand' (cited in Johnston 37–8).

13 The author of *Flora Lyndsay* implies that she is the same person as the author of *Roughing It* on the last page of the book. See Fowler, *ET*, 103, for additional evidence that the novel is autobiographical.

14 'The Ould Dragoon,' 'The Land-Jobber,' and 'The Village Hotel' appear in the first 1852 edition; 'Canadian Sketches' was added to the second.

3: Translated by Desire

1 See Gerson, *A Purer Taste*, for a comprehensive account of the arguments used in favour of historical fiction in both pre- and post-Confederation periods.

2 See Gerson, *A Purer Taste*, chapter 8.

3 'Parkman almost single-handedly determined the direction of Canadian historiography and historical fiction for the last three decades of the nineteenth century' (Gerson, *A Purer Taste* 113).

4 See Gerson, *A Purer Taste*, 52.

5 See, for example, comments on the limitations of romance as a genre in Mary Jane Edwards, 'Novels in English: Beginnings to 1900' (567–8); and Cal Smiley, 'Novels in English: 1900 to 1920' (570–1) in the *Oxford Companion to Canadian Literature*; see also comments on reading literature to discover the 'real lives' of women in MacMillan, McMullen, and Waterston, *Silenced Sextet*; and Helen Buss, *Mapping Our Selves* (*passim*).

6 See also Stockdale, 'Introduction,' xiii.

7 Stockdale's introduction points out that during 1863–4, when Leprohon wrote the novel, Montreal's being flooded with English soldiers preparing for a possible invasion from the United States reproduced the circumstances of the 1760s depicted in the book and thus rendered it highly topical to its contemporary audience (xi–xii). However, the bulk of his introduction goes to great lengths to find historical sources for the secret marriage, the duel, and the

family histories depicted in the book. While his specific findings seem plausible, the whole exercise seems wrong-headed; why would Leprohon have found it necessary to justify including a secret marriage or a duel by reference to 'reality'? These were standard plot elements of British novels from the supposedly 'realistic' Dickens to popular sensation fiction; *Une femme de trentes ans*, by Balzac, which Stockdale and Edwards identify as a major influence on the novel, includes as a major character a pirate queen dripping in jewels and such plot elements as two coincidental family reunions and a lasting happy marriage based on love at first sight between a felon and an upper-class teenager. (See Edwards, 'Essentially Canadian,' 9; and Stockdale, 'Introduction,' xxxiv. Dickens was also clearly an influence, as stated in *Armand Durand*.) The imperative to link *Antoinette* to material reality seems to be Stockdale's, not Leprohon's, and it indicates his modernist prejudice in favour of realism and against romance, no matter how successful.

8 Carole Gerson notes the use of 'national allegory' (*A Purer Taste* 120) in 'the frequency of marriages between *belles Québécoises* and valiant Englishmen in nineteenth-century English-Canadian fiction,' suggesting that 'the sexual submission of the individual symbolis[es] the political submission of the group' (*A Purer Taste* 120). My interpretation does not contradict, but rather elaborates on, Gerson's, by suggesting that *Antoinette* uses the 'sexual contract' to empower the feminine sphere and to create a fiction of equality between the two groups.

9 Armstrong, *passim*.

10 Gerson and Stockdale have pointed out that contemporary critics faulted *Antoinette* because it presented French-Canadian women as eager to marry Englishmen. Gerson cites 'reviewers for both *L'Ordre* and *La Revue Canadienne*' who 'disliked the "anglomanie" implicit in Mrs. D'Aulnay's eagerness to greet "avec tant d'empressement les militaires étrangers, et ouvrir ses salons à ceux-là même qui auraient dû être les derniers admis"' ('Three Writers of Victorian Canada' 213). See Stockdale, Introduction, xxxix–xl. While the critics made this point, the novel does not.

11 Chapter 5 contains a paraphrase of the history of the Conquest and its aftermath taken primarily from Garneau, according to Stockdale.

4: Explain Yourself

1 See Bacchi, 26.

2 A useful collection of such articles can be found in Cook and Mitchinson, *The Proper Sphere*.

3 For discussions of New Woman fiction in Britain and the United States, see

Lyn Pykett, *The 'Improper' Feminine*; Penny Boumelha, *Thomas Hardy and Women*; Elaine Showalter, *A Literature of Their Own* and *Sexual Anarchy*; and Elaine Showalter, ed. *Daughters of Decadence*.

4 These terms were adapted by Carol Bacchi from Aileen Kraditor's study of the U.S. suffrage movement, which uses 'feminism' and 'social feminism' (or social reform) to distinguish between the early U.S. suffrage movement based in the principles of the American Declaration of Independence and articulated in the Seneca Falls declaration of 1848, and the later movement which (Kraditor argues) from the 1880s onward took a more conservative position in response to American anxiety over immigration and the debate over 'slave' and 'free' states. The history of first-wave feminism in Canada is quite different. Though there were a few feminists who could be characterized solely as proponents of 'equal rights,' English-Canadian women (as well as men) generally rejected the 'equal rights' argument at the time it was made, as part and parcel of the Republicanism they deplored. Feminist activism in Canada begins in the period Kraditor identifies as conservative; not surprisingly, Canadian feminists were part of a mainstream consensus of political thought which held that a hierarchically organized society was unavoidable, that Anglo-Saxons were superior to other 'races,' and that both government and the rich were obligated to intervene in social and economic institutions to mitigate the worst excesses of capitalism. However, these views were not a conservative backlash against an earlier equal rights rhetoric, but a consistent development of English-Canadian thought from the early nineteenth century. Thus, many recent commentaries have questioned the usefulness of framing the history of Canadian feminism in terms of a debate between equal rights and maternal feminism; Canadians, in fact, seemed not to distinguish between the two.

5 See Russett, *Sexual Science, passim*, for an exposition of the way these four principles were used to justify women's subordinate position in society.

6 As I have argued in my 'Introduction' to the Tecumseh edition of Sara Jeannette Duncan's *A Daughter of Today*, even Elfrida Bell, the 'daughter' of the *fin de siècle*, abandons her sexless stance and desires marriage (xiv).

7 Carrie MacMillan argues in *Silenced Sextet* that Judith represents 'art' and so the resolution of the plot in Judith's return to rural Ontario is an allegorical representation of the indigenizing of art. However, the representation of Judith's singing as 'natural' rather than cultural, and the fact that Andrew forbids Judith to sing in public after she becomes his wife, argue against this reading. See *Silenced Sextet*, 184–90.

8 Carrie MacMillan (*Silenced Sextet* 175) points out the way that Jamestown functions as a precursor of other Canadian literary small towns.

9 Russett details the specifics of the concept of degeneration, which in evolutionary theory had the specific meaning of a movement downward on an evolutionary scale.

10 Lorraine McMullen notes that in Dougall's work, receptivity to scenery and the moral values it symbolizes is an index of moral worth ('Lily Dougall's Vision' 142).

11 Carrie MacMillan discusses the discrepancy between Dorothy's intellectual understanding and her emotional craving for love as an example of the feminine 'divided self.' See 'Introduction,' xi–xiv.

12 Lyn Pykett also argues that the New Woman novel is a self-conscious response to the woman question (7). Sandra Campbell argues that because each of the characters in the stories seems to be telling her story to the narrator, the 'real communication in them is usually between *woman* and *woman*' (ix). I would argue, in contrast, that this technique allows the reader, male or female, to overhear the intimate conversation between women, which is usually protected, and thereby to witness women more fully revealed to the male listener.

5: Voicing the Voiceless

1 Carol Bacchi notes that the maternal feminist conformity to the domestic stereotype 'may have been rhetoric ... But the consistency with which the new suffragists not only accepted but eulogized woman's domestic duties suggests that they genuinely believed in the sexual division of labour' (33–4). Randi Warne argues at length that McClung's endorsement of women's domestic role was a rhetorical strategy designed to counter specific arguments from her opposition, and cannot be identified with her actual views (85–135). I would argue that in the absence of the author, it is impossible to judge exactly which texts represent her actual views, if indeed she held consistent, logically related views throughout her entire lifetime in every situation; we are limited to texts, and we cannot infer the presence of the author from them. However, this controversy is instructive for the way it points out the contradictions inherent in heterosexual feminist ideology.

2 Bacchi, following Aileen Kraditor's study of the U.S. suffrage movement, differentiates between 'feminists' and 'social reformers' among the suffragists, placing McClung squarely in the latter category (32–3). Veronica Strong-Boag argues forcefully for McClung's feminism, suggesting that by calling for the vote women demanded 'a direct relationship to the state as individuals,' which gained women the 'potential to use the state to alter the balance of power between the sexes in the home and the world at large' ('Ever a Crusader' 311–12). Warne also opposes what she styles Bacchi's 'liberal' views by attempting to define a feminism which includes McClung's religious beliefs.

3 See, for example, A.B. McKillop, *A Disciplined Intelligence*; Leslie Armour, *The Idea of Canada*; or R.D. Mathews, *Canadian Literature: Surrender or Revolution*.

4 Warne notes: 'McClung ... employed the technique of "reversal" ... She simply quoted her opponents against themselves' (119).

5 Mariana Valverde's discussion of cleanliness as a metaphor for moral purity shows how the two were associated; her analysis of the 'dishwashing' metaphor used by the social purity movement (40) is important context for the dishwashing scene in *Painted Fires* (17–19).

6 Carolyn Strange's book on the 'girl problem' offers a useful context for understanding the moral problem that single girls, like those resident in the 'Girl's Friendly Home,' were supposed to pose, and the ways that McClung and her political allies proposed to solve that problem through groups like the CGIT and the YMCA.

7 Helmi's fate is part of a complex discourse surrounding immigration in Canada at the turn of the century. McClung's novel seems to argue that rather than becoming a potentially disruptive 'fallen woman,' the single immigrant woman was more likely to become a victim of corrupt elements in Canadian society. 'Home Mission' groups associated with the Methodist Church as well as many voluntary and philanthropic groups set themselves to police and regulate the sexual lives of immigrant women, as well as to 'Canadianize' them by inculcating Protestant values. See Valverde 104–28. McClung sidesteps the issue of race by making her immigrant both 'white' and representative of the 'northern races.'

8 McClung's fiction generally falls into the category of the 'domestic family novel' popular in the first decades of the twentieth century, which 'recounted the growing up and first love experiences of a child or family in a manner notable for its excess of "syrupy pathos, sentiment and optimism"' (J.D. Hart, cited in Vipond, 'Bestsellers ... 1899–1918' 104).

9 See Misao Dean, *A Different Point of View*, 19–40, for a discussion of the way Duncan breaks with literary convention (for her, associated with England) in order to express 'colonial reality.'

10 Mary Hallett and Marilyn Davis name this strategy 'antiromantic'; their analysis differs from mine in asserting that the 'real' which is generated in opposition to 'romance' in McClung's fiction constitutes actual physical reality. See Hallett and Davis, 228–69.

11 Elizabeth Thompson discusses *Painted Fires* and *Purple Springs* in her section on McClung (*The Pioneer Woman* 83–7).

12 See Deborah Gorham's discussion of the connection between 'Nellie's' feminism and the depiction of her mother in *Clearing in the West*. However, in this article, Gorham assumes that the incidents in the book are simple fact, and equates the persona with McClung herself.

6: Femininity and the Real in *As for Me and My House*

1 See April Alliston, 'Female Sexuality and the Referent of Enlightenment Realisms,' 13, on the importance of firsthand accounts in establishing the 'truth' of classic realist texts. Catherine Belsey argues that in the classic realist novel the privileged interpretive comments of the narrator are the reader's guarantee of the mimetic truth of the text: 'the reader is invited to perceive and judge the "truth" of the text, the coherent, non-contradictory interpretation of the world as it is perceived by the [narrator] whose autonomy is the source and evidence of the truth of the interpretation' (Belsey 68–9).

2 Paul Denham points out that there is in fact little detailed commentary on domestic chores, noting the omission of sewing clothes from Mrs Bentley's housewifely accomplishments, and the sketchiness of the meals she serves. His argument that the garden in the novel has become wholly symbolic is persuasive; however, some of his points seem designed to buttress the argument that Mrs Bentley is not a nice person. His article suggests that he knows a lot more about women's work in a Prairie town than Ross did.

3 See Barbara Godard, 'El Greco in Canada,' 124–32.

4 See ibid.

5 Dennis Cooley notes that Mrs Bentley takes it upon herself 'to name "the real Philip"' (108).

6 See David Williams, 'The "Scarlet" Rompers,' for a convincing argument that the novel presents Philip as an effective and happy minister.

7 David Stouck, Ross's biographer, confirms that Ross avidly read what Freud and Ellis he could procure at public libraries and ordered other texts by mail, which arrived in a plain cover to avoid censorship. Ross's recently revealed ambivalence about his own sexuality (see Fraser) may have motivated this reading, as it did for many other gay and bisexual intellectuals in the early twentieth century.

8 For the role of the recognition of castration in creating as part of femininity a sense of inferiority, an obsession with appearance, contempt for and jealousy of women, see Freud, 'Some Psychical Consequences of the Anatomical Distinction between the Sexes': 'After a woman has become aware of the wound to her narcissism, she develops, like a scar, a sense of inferiority. When she has passed beyond her first attempt at explaining her lack of a penis as being a punishment personal to herself and has realised that sexual character is a universal one, she begins to share the contempt felt by men for a sex which is the lesser in so important a respect, and, at least in holding that opinion, insist on being like a man. Even after penis envy has abandoned its true object, it continues to exist: by an easy displacement it persists in the character trait of *jealousy*' (674).

9 Critics have attributed the baby variously to Paul (David Williams) and to Mr Finley (Evelyn Hinz and John Teunissen) as well as to Philip Bentley.

10 See Stouck, 'The Mirror and the Lamp': 'his aversion for his mother extends to all women' (97).

11 See Helen Buss, 'Who Are You,' 191, for a compendium of the various charges.

12 In his Afterword to *As for Me and My House*, Kroetsch characterizes the novel as a 'splendid dance of evasions' (221). In 'Sinclair Ross's Ambivalent World,' W.H. New argues that the novel is constructed to create ambivalence in the reader about how to judge the characters (49).

13 See Lorraine McMullen, *Sinclair Ross*, 22.

14 See Buss, 'Who Are You?' 191–2. Robert Kroetsch, in 'The Fear of Women in Prairie Fiction: An Erotics of Space,' suggests that the novel is organized by a system of masculine and feminine binaries which are summed up in the opposition horse/house. He argues that masculinity as defined in Prairie novels is essentially silent, solitary, and oriented towards external space, while femininity is domestic, confined, and spoken; the failure of the two to meet in the traditional garden or whorehouse represents the refusal of the man to give up his essence, to 'make the radical change' which marriage would require (120).

Works Cited

Alliston, April. 'Female Sexuality and the Referent of Enlightenment Realisms.' In *Spectacles of Realism*. Ed. Margaret Cohen and Christopher Prendergast. Minneapolis: U of Minnesota P, 1995. 11–27.

Armour, Leslie. *The Idea of Canada*. Ottawa: Steel Rail, 1982.

Armstrong, Nancy. *Desire and Domestic Fiction: A Political History of the Novel*. New York: Oxford UP, 1987.

Atwood, Margaret. *The Journals of Susanna Moodie*. Toronto: Oxford UP, 1970.

– *Survival: A Thematic Guide to Canadian Literature*. Toronto: Anansi, 1972.

Bacchi, Carol Lee. *Liberation Deferred? The Ideas of the English-Canadian Suffragists, 1887–1918*. Toronto: U of Toronto P, 1983.

Ballstadt, Carl. 'Catharine Parr Traill.' In *Canadian Writers and Their Works: Fiction Series*. Vol. 1. Ed. Robert Lecker, Jack David, and Ellen Quigley. Downsview, Ont.: ECW Press, 1983. 149–94.

– Editor's Introduction. *Roughing It in the Bush*, by Susanna Moodie. Ottawa: Carleton UP, 1988.

– Introduction. *The Canadian Settler's Guide*. Vancouver: Alcuin Society, 1971.

– 'Susanna Moodie and the English Sketch.' *Canadian Literature* 51 (Winter 1972): 32–8.

Balzac, Honoré de. *A Woman of Thirty*. 'Édition définitif' of the *Comédie Humaine*. Vol. 18. Trans. George Burnham Ives. Philadelphia: George Barrie, 1897.

Barrett, Michèle. *The Politics of Truth: From Marx to Foucault*. Stanford: Stanford UP, 1991.

Barthes, Roland. 'Myth Today.' In *The Barthes Reader*. Ed. Susan Sontag. New York: Hill and Wang, 1982. 93–149.

Beer, Gillian. *Darwin's Plots: Evolutionary Narrative in Darwin, George Eliot and Nineteenth-Century Fiction*. London: Routledge, 1983.

Belsey, Catherine. *Critical Practice*. London: Routledge, 1980.

Bentley, David. Afterword. *The Backwoods of Canada*, by Catharine Parr Traill. Toronto: McClelland and Stewart, 1989. 291–301.

– 'Breaking the "Cake of Custom": The Atlantic Crossing as a Rubicon for Female Emigrants to Canada?' In *Re(Dis)covering our Foremothers: Nineteenth-Century Canadian Women Writers*. Ed. Lorraine McMullen. Ottawa: U of Ottawa P, 1990. 91–122.

Boumelha, Penny. *Thomas Hardy and Women: Sexual Ideology and Narrative Form*. Madison: U of Wisconsin P, 1985.

Buss, Helen. 'Canadian Women's Autobiography: Some Critical Directions.' In *A Mazing Space: Writing Canadian Women Writing*. Ed. Shirley Neuman and Smaro Kamboureli. Edmonton: Longspoon/NeWest P, 1986. 154–64.

– *Mapping Our Selves: Canadian Women's Autobiography in English*. Montreal: McGill-Queen's UP, 1993.

– 'Who Are You, Mrs. Bentley: Feminist Re-vision and Sinclair Ross's *As for Me and My House*' (1990). In *Sinclair Ross's 'As for Me and My House': Five Decades of Criticism*. Ed. David Stouck. Toronto: U of Toronto P, 1991. 190–208.

Butler, Judith. *Bodies That Matter: On the Discursive Limits of 'Sex.'* New York: Routledge, 1993.

– *Gender Trouble: Feminism and the Subversion of Identity*. New York: Routledge, 1990.

Cady, Edwin. *The Light of Common Day: Realism in American Fiction*. Bloomington: Indiana UP, 1971.

Campbell, Sandra. Introduction. *Sister Woman*, by Jessie Sime. 1919. Ottawa: Tecumseh, 1992. vii–xxxv.

Campbell, Sandra, and Lorraine McMullen, eds. *New Women: Short Stories by Canadian Women 1900–1920*. Ottawa: U of Ottawa P, 1991.

Cheney, Harriet V. *The Rivals of Acadia*. Boston: Wells and Lily, 1827.

Cleverdon, C.L. *The Woman Suffrage Movement in Canada*. 1950. Toronto: U of Toronto P, 1974.

Cohen, Marjorie Griffin. *Women's Work, Markets, and Economic Development in Nineteenth-Century Ontario*. Toronto: U of Toronto P, 1988.

Cook, Ramsay, and Wendy Mitchinson, eds. *The Proper Sphere: Women's Place in Canadian Society*. Toronto: Oxford UP, 1976.

Cooley, Dennis. 'An Awful Stumbling Toward Names: Ross and the (Un)Common Noun.' In *From the Heart of the Heartland: The Fiction of Sinclair Ross*. Ed. John Moss. Ottawa: U of Ottawa P, 1992. 103–24.

Cude, Wilfred. 'Beyond Mrs. Bentley: A Study of *As for Me and My House*' (1973). In *Sinclair Ross's 'As for Me and My House': Five Decades of Criticism*. Ed. David Stouck. Toronto: U of Toronto P, 1991. 76–95.

Daniells, Roy. 'Introduction' (1957). In *Sinclair Ross's 'As for Me and My House': Five Decades of Criticism*. Ed. David Stouck. Toronto: U of Toronto P, 1991. 35–40.

Davey, Frank. 'The Conflicting Signs of *As for Me and My House*' (1990). In *Sinclair*

Ross's 'As for Me and My House': Five Decades of Criticism. Ed. David Stouck. Toronto: U of Toronto P, 1991. 178–90.

Deacon, William Arthur. 'Story of a Prairie Parson's Wife' (1941). In *Sinclair Ross's 'As for Me and My House': Five Decades of Criticism*. Ed. David Stouck. Toronto: U of Toronto P, 1991. 18–19.

Dean, Misao. *A Different Point of View: Sara Jeannette Duncan*. Montreal: McGill-Queen's UP, 1991.

de Lauretis, Teresa. *The Practice of Love: Lesbian Sexuality and Perverse Desire*. Bloomington: Indiana UP, 1994.

Denham, Paul. 'Narrative Technique in Sinclair Ross's *As for Me and My House*.' *Studies in Canadian Literature* 5.1 (Spring 1980): 116–24.

Dougall, Lily. *The Madonna of a Day*. New York: D. Appleton, 1895.

Duncan, Sara Jeannette. *A Daughter of Today*. 1894. Intro. Misao Dean. Ottawa: Tecumseh, 1988.

– 'Saunterings.' *Week* 3.48 (20 Oct. 1886): 771–2.

DuPlessis, Rachel Blau. *Writing beyond the Ending: Narrative Strategies of Twentieth-Century Women Writers*. Bloomington: Indiana UP, 1985.

Durning, Simon. Introduction. *The Cultural Studies Reader*. London: Routledge, 1993. 1–25.

Easthope, Antony. *Literary into Cultural Studies*. London: Routledge, 1991.

'The Editor's Shanty.' Rev. of *The Female Emigrant's Guide*, by Catharine Parr Traill. *Anglo-American Magazine* 6.2 (1855): 220.

'The Editor's Shanty.' Rev. of *The Female Emigrant's Guide*, by Catharine Parr Traill. *Anglo-American Magazine* 6.4 (1855): 386–9.

Edwards, Mary Jane. 'Essentially Canadian.' *Canadian Literature* 52 (Spring 1972): 8–23.

– 'Novels in English: Beginnings to 1900.' In *Oxford Companion to Canadian Literature*. Ed. William Toye. Toronto: Oxford UP, 1983. 565–9.

– 'Rosanna Leprohon.' In *Oxford Companion to Canadian Literature*. Ed. William Toye. Toronto: Oxford UP, 1983. 449–50.

Egerton, George. 'A Keynote to Keynotes.' In *Ten Contemporaries*. Ed. John Gawsworth. London: Ernest Benn, 1932.

Esterhammer, Angela. '"Can't See Life for Illusions": The Problematic Realism of Sinclair Ross.' In *From the Heart of the Heartland: The Fiction of Sinclair Ross*. Ed. John Moss. Ottawa: U of Ottawa P, 1992. 15–23.

Felski, Rita. *Beyond Feminist Aesthetics: Feminist Literature and Social Change*. Cambridge: Harvard UP, 1989.

'Female Influence upon Religion.' *Instructor* 5 (27 May 1835): 35.

'Forest Life in Canada West.' Rev. of *Roughing It in the Bush*, by Susanna Moodie. *Blackwoods* 71 (March 1852): 355–65.

Foucault, Michel. *The History of Sexuality.* Vol. 1. *An Introduction.* Trans. Robert Hurley. New York: Random House, 1990.

Fowler, Marian. *The Embroidered Tent: Five Gentlewomen in Upper Canada.* Toronto: Anansi, 1982.

– 'Roughing It in the Bush: A Sentimental Novel.' In *Beginnings: The Canadian Novel, a Critical Anthology.* Ed. John Moss. Toronto: NC Press, 1980. 80–96.

Fraser, Keath. 'As for Me and My Secrets.' *Saturday Night,* March 1997, 75–80.

Freiwald, Bina. '"The Tongue of Woman": The Language of the Self in Moodie's *Roughing It in the Bush.*' In *Re(Dis)covering Our Foremothers: Nineteenth-Century Canadian Women Writers.* Ed. Lorraine McMullen. Ottawa: U of Ottawa P, 1990. 155–72.

French, Sarah. *Letters to a Young Lady on Leaving School and Entering the World.* Boston: Crosby, Nichols, 1855.

Freud, Sigmund. 'Female Sexuality.' In *The Standard Edition of the Complete Psychological Works of Sigmund Freud.* Vol. 21. Trans. James Strachey. London: Hogarth Press, 1961. 225–43.

– 'Femininity.' In *The Standard Edition of the Complete Psychological Works of Sigmund Freud.* Vol. 22. Trans. James Strachey. London: Hogarth Press, 1964. 112–35.

– 'Some Psychical Consequences of the Anatomical Distinction between the Sexes.' In *The Freud Reader.* Ed. Peter Gay. New York: Norton, 1989. 670–8.

Frye, Northrop. 'Conclusion to *A Literary History of Canada.*' In *The Bush Garden: Essays on the Canadian Imagination.* Toronto: Anansi, 1971. 213–51.

Fytche, Maria Amelia. *Kerchiefs to Hunt Souls.* 1895. Intro. Carrie MacMillan. Sackville, N.B.: Ralph Pickard Bell Library, 1980.

Gairdner, William. 'Traill and Moodie: The Two Realities.' *Journal of Canadian Fiction* 1.2 (Spring 1972): 35–42.

G.B. 'Prairie Main Street' (1941). In *Sinclair Ross's 'As for Me and My House': Five Decades of Criticism.* Ed. David Stouck. Toronto: U of Toronto P, 1991. 15–16.

Genette, Gérard. *Narrative Discourse: An Essay in Method.* Trans. Jane E. Lewin. Ithaca, N.Y.: Cornell UP 1980.

Gerson, Carole. *A Purer Taste: The Writing and Reading of Fiction in English in Nineteenth-Century Canada.* Toronto: U of Toronto P, 1989.

– 'Three Writers of Victorian Canada.' In *Canadian Writers and Their Works: Fiction Series.* Vol. 1. Ed. Robert Lecker, Jack David, and Ellen Quigley. Downsview, Ont.: ECW Press, 1983. 195–256.

Gilbert, Sandra, and Susan Gubar. *No Man's Land: The Place of the Woman Writer in the Twentieth Century.* Vol. 1. *The War of the Words.* New Haven: Yale UP, 1988.

Glickman, Susan. 'The Waxing and Waning of Susanna Moodie's "Enthusiasm."' *Canadian Literature* 130 (Autumn 1991): 7–28.

Godard, Barbara. 'El Greco in Canada: Sinclair Ross's *'As for Me and My House'* (1981). In *Sinclair Ross's 'As for Me and My House': Five Decades of Criticism*. Ed. Stouck. Toronto: U of Toronto P, 1991. 120–37.

– 'A Portrait with Three Faces: The New Woman in Fiction by Canadian Women, 1880–1920.' *Literary Criterion* 19.3–4 (1984): 72–92.

Gorham, Deborah. 'The Canadian Suffragists.' In *Women in the Canadian Mosaic*. Ed. Gwen Matheson. Toronto: Peter Martin Associates, 1976. 23–56.

Hallett, Mary, and Marilyn I. Davis. *Firing the Heather: The Life and Times of Nellie McClung*. Saskatoon: Fifth House Publishers, 1994.

Herbert, Mary Elizabeth. *Woman as She Should Be*. Halifax: M.E. Herbert, 1861.

Hinz, Evelyn, and John Teunissen. 'Who's the Father of Mrs. Bentley's Child? *As for Me and My House* and the Conventions of the Dramatic Monologue' (1986). In *Sinclair Ross's 'As for Me and My House': Five Decades of Criticism*. Ed. David Stouck. Toronto: U of Toronto P, 1991. 148–61.

Jackel, David. 'Mrs. Moodie and Mrs. Traill and the Fabrication of a Canadian Tradition.' *Compass* 6 (1979): 1–22.

Jackel, Susan. 'Canadian Women's Autobiography: A Problem of Criticism.' In *Gynocritics: Feminist Approaches to Canadian and Quebec Women's Writing*. Ed. Barbara Godard. Toronto: ECW Press, 1987. 97–110.

Jennings, Miss Clothilde. *The White Rose of Acadia*. Halifax: J. Bowes, 1855.

Johnston, Judith. '"Woman's Testimony": Imperialist Discourse in the Professional Colonial Travel Writing of Louisa Anne Meredith and Catharine Parr Traill.' *Australian and New Zealand Studies in Canada* (June 1994): 34–55.

Klinck, Carl. Introduction. *Antoinette de Mirecourt; or, Secret Marrying and Secret Sorrowing*, by Rosanna Leprohon. Toronto: McClelland and Stewart, 1973.

– Introduction. *Roughing It in the Bush*, by Susanna Moodie. Toronto: McClelland and Stewart, 1962.

Kroetsch, Robert. Afterword. *As for Me and My House*, by Sinclair Ross. Toronto: McClelland and Stewart, 1989. 217–21

– 'The Fear of Women in Prairie Fiction: An Erotics of Space' (1979). In *Sinclair Ross's 'As for Me and My House': Five Decades of Criticism*. Ed. David Stouck. Toronto: U of Toronto P, 1991. 111–20.

Ladha, Yasmin. 'Circum the Gesture.' *Open Letter* 9.3 (Summer 1995): 59.

Lecker, Robert. *Making It Real: The Canonisation of English-Canadian Literature*. Toronto: Anansi, 1995.

Leprohon, Rosanna. 'Alice Sydenham's First Ball' (1849). In *Pioneering Women: Short Stories by Canadian Women*. Ed. Lorraine McMullen and Sandra Campbell. Ottawa: U of Ottawa P, 1993. 155–88.

– *Antoinette de Mirecourt; or, Secret Marrying and Secret Sorrowing*. Ed. John Stockdale. Ottawa: Carleton UP, 1989.

– *Armand Durand; or, A Promise Fulfilled.* Montreal: Lovell, 1868.
– *The Manor House of de Villerai.* Ed John Robert Sorfleet. *Journal of Canadian Fiction* 34 (1985): 13–151.
McClung, Nellie L. *All We like Sheep and Other Stories.* Toronto: Thomas Allen, 1926.
– *Be Good to Yourself.* Toronto: Thomas Allen, 1930.
– *Clearing in the West, My Own Story.* 1935. Toronto: Thomas Allen, 1976.
– *In Times like These.* Intro. Veronica Strong-Boag. Toronto: U of Toronto P, 1972.
– *Leaves from Lantern Lane.* Toronto: Thomas Allen, 1936.
– *Painted Fires.* Toronto: Ryerson Press, 1925.
– *Purple Springs.* Toronto: Thomas Allen, 1921.
– *The Second Chance.* Toronto: Ryerson, 1910.
– *Sowing Seeds in Danny.* Toronto: William Briggs, 1908.
– *The Stream Runs Fast.* Toronto: Thomas Allen, 1945.
McDonald, Larry. 'I Looked for It, and There It Was – Gone: History in Postmodern Criticism.' *ECW* 56 (Fall 1995): 37–50.
McDonald, Mary Lu. 'Susanna Moodie: The Patrick Hamilton Ewing Collection of Moodie–Strickland–Vickers–Ewing Family Papers.' *National Library News* 19.12 (Dec. 1987): 1–5.
MacDonald, R.D. 'Design and Purpose.' *Canadian Literature* 51 (1972): 20–31.
McKillop, A.B. *A Disciplined Intelligence.* Montreal: McGill-Queen's UP, 1979.
MacLulich, T.D. 'Crusoe in the Backwoods: A Canadian Fable?' *Mosaic* 9.2 (1976): 115–26.
McMaster, Susan, ed. *Two Women Talking: Correspondence 1985 to 1987; Erin Mouré and Bronwen Wallace.* Toronto: Feminist Caucus of the League of Canadian Poets, 1993.
MacMillan, Carrie. Introduction. *Kerchiefs to Hunt Souls,* by Maria Amelia Fytche. Sackville, N.B.: Ralph Pickard Bell Library, 1980. i–xxi.
MacMillan, Carrie, Lorraine McMullen, and Elizabeth Waterston. *Silenced Sextet: Six Nineteenth-Century Canadian Women Novelists.* Montreal: McGill-Queen's UP, 1992.
McMullen, Lorraine. 'Lily Dougall's Vision of Canada.' In *A Mazing Space.* Ed. Shirley Neuman and Smaro Kamboureli. Edmonton: Longspoon/NeWest, 1986. 137–47.
– *Sinclair Ross.* Boston: G.K. Hall, 1979.
McMullen, Lorraine, and Sandra Campbell, eds. *Pioneering Women: Short Stories by Canadian Women, Beginnings to 1880.* Ottawa: U of Ottawa P, 1993.
Marlatt, Daphne. *Ana Historic.* Toronto: Coach House, 1988.
– *Taken.* Toronto: Anansi, 1996.
Mason, Mary G. 'The Other Voice: Autobiographies of Women Writers.' In *Autobiography, Essays Theoretical and Critical.* Ed. James Olney. Princeton: Princeton UP, 1980. 207–35.

Mathews, R.D. *Canadian Literature: Surrender or Revolution.* Toronto: Steel Rail, 1978.

Mitchinson, Wendy. *The Nature of Their Bodies: Women and Their Doctors in Victorian Canada.* Toronto: U of Toronto P, 1991.

– 'The WCTU: For God, Home and Native Land.' In *A Not Unreasonable Claim: Women and Reform in Canada, 1880s–1920s.* Ed. Linda Kealey. Toronto: Women's Press, 1979. 151–67.

Moodie, Susanna. 'The Broken Mirror.' In *Voyages: Short Narratives of Susanna Moodie.* Ed. John Thurston. Ottawa: U of Ottawa P, 1991. 64–86.

– *Enthusiasm; and Other Poems.* London: Smith Elder and Co., 1831.

– *Flora Lyndsay.* New York: Dewitt and Davenport, n.d.

– *Letters of Love and Duty: The Correspondence of Susanna and John Moodie.* Ed. Carl Ballstadt, Elizabeth Hopkins, and Michael Peterman. Toronto: U of Toronto P, 1993.

– *Life in the Clearings.* Ed. Robert L. McDougall. Toronto: Macmillan, 1959.

– 'Rachel Wilde; or, Trifles from the Burthen of a Life.' In *Voyages: Short Narratives of Susanna Moodie* Ed. John Thurston. Ottawa: U of Ottawa P, 1991. 98–150.

– *Roughing It in the Bush.* 1st ed. London: Bentley, 1852.

– *Roughing It in the Bush.* Ed. Carl Ballstadt. Ottawa: Carleton UP, 1988.

– *Roughing It in the Bush.* 2nd ed. with additions. London: Bentley, 1852; rpt. Toronto: McClelland and Stewart, 1989.

– *Susanna Moodie: Letters of a Lifetime.* Ed. Carl Ballstadt, Elizabeth Hopkins, and Michael Peterman. Toronto: U of Toronto P, 1985.

– 'Trifles from the Burthen of a Life.' In *Voyages: Short Narratives of Susanna Moodie.* Ed. John Thurston. Ottawa: U of Ottawa P, 1991. 160–240.

– 'Well in the Wilderness.' In *Voyages: Short Narratives of Susanna Moodie.* Ed. John Thurston. Ottawa: U of Ottawa P, 1991. 87–97.

Moss, John. 'Mrs. Bentley and the Bicameral Mind: A Hermeneutical Encounter with *As for Me and My House*' (1982). In *Sinclair Ross's 'As for Me and My House': Five Decades of Criticism.* Ed. David Stouck. Toronto: U of Toronto P, 1991. 138–47.

New, W.H. 'Sinclair Ross's Ambivalent World' (1969). *Sinclair Ross's 'As for Me and My House': Five Decades of Criticism.* Ed. David Stouck. Toronto: U of Toronto P, 1991. 48–54.

Peterman, Michael. 'In Search of Agnes Strickland's Sisters.' *Canadian Literature* 121 (Summer 1989): 115–24.

– 'Splendid Anachronism: The Record of Catharine Parr Traill's Struggles as an Amateur Botanist in Nineteenth-Century Canada.' In *Re(Dis)covering Our Foremothers: Nineteenth-Century Canadian Women Writers.* Ed. Lorraine McMullen. Ottawa: U of Ottawa P, 1990. 173–85.

Poovey, Mary. *The Proper Lady and the Woman Writer: Ideology as Style in the Works of Mary Wollstonecraft, Mary Shelley, and Jane Austen.* Chicago: U of Chicago P, 1984.

Pratt, Mary. *Mary Pratt.* Intro. Sandra Gwyn. Commentary by Gerda Moray. Toronto: McGraw-Hill Ryerson, 1989.

Prentice, Alison, et al. *Canadian Women: A History.* Toronto: Harcourt Brace Jovanovich, 1988.

Pykett, Lyn. *The 'Improper' Feminine: The Women's Sensation Novel and the New Woman Writing.* London: Routledge, 1992.

Rev. of *The Backwoods of Canada,* by Catharine Parr Traill. *Athenaeum,* 20 February 1836, 138–9.

Rev. of *The Canadian House-keeper's Guide,* by Catharine Parr Traill. *Irish Canadian* 3.13 (5 April 1865): 5.

Rev. of *The Female Emigrant's Guide,* by Catharine Parr Traill. *Maple Leaf* 4.12 (Dec. 1854): 379–80.

Rev. of *Roughing It in the Bush,* by Susanna Moodie. *Athenaeum,* 28 February 1852, 247–8.

Ricou, Laurence. 'The Prairie Internalised: The Fiction of Sinclair Ross' (1973). In *Sinclair Ross's 'As for Me and My House': Five Decades of Criticism.* Ed. David Stouck. Toronto: U of Toronto P, 1991. 66–75.

Ross, Morton. 'The Canonization of *As for Me and My House*: A Case Study.' In *Figures in a Ground: Canadian Essays on Modern Literature Collected in Honor of Sheila Watson.* Ed. Diane Bessai and David Jackel. Saskatoon: Western Producer Prairie Books, 1978. 189–205.

Ross, Sinclair. *As for Me and My House.* 1941. Afterword by Robert Kroetsch. Toronto: McClelland and Stewart, 1989.

Russett, Cynthia Eagle. *Sexual Science: The Victorian Construction of Womanhood.* Cambridge: Harvard UP, 1989.

Shields, Carol. *Susanna Moodie: Voice and Vision.* Ottawa: Borealis Press, 1977.

Showalter, Elaine. *Sexual Anarchy: Gender and Culture at the Fin de Siècle.* New York: Viking, 1990.

– ed. *Daughters of Decadence: Women Writers of the Fin de Siècle.* New Brunswick, N.J.: Rutgers UP, 1993.

– *A Literature of Their Own: British Women Novelists from Bronte to Lessing.* Princeton: Princeton UP, 1977.

Sime, Jessie. *Sister Woman.* 1919. Intro. Sandra Campbell. Ottawa: Tecumseh, 1992.

Smiley, Cal. 'Novels in English: 1900 to 1920.' In *Oxford Companion to Canadian Literature.* Ed. William Toye. Toronto: Oxford UP, 1983. 569–71.

Smith, Sidonie. *A Poetics of Women's Autobiography.* Bloomington: Indiana UP, 1987.

Sorfleet, John Robert. Introduction. *The Manor House of de Villerai,* by Mrs J.L. Leprohon. *Journal of Canadian Fiction* 34 (1985): 3–12.

Spacks, Patricia Meyer. *Gossip*. New York: Alfred Knopf, 1985.

– 'Reflecting Women.' *Yale Review* 63.1 (Oct. 1973): 26–42.

Stanton, Domna. 'Autogynography: Is the Subject Different?' In *The Female Autograph*. Ed. Domna Stanton. Chicago: U of Chicago P, 1987. 3–20.

Stead, W.T. 'The Novel of the Modern Woman.' *Review of Reviews*, 18 July 1894, 64–74.

Stockdale, John. Introduction. *Antoinette de Mirecourt*, by Rosanna Leprohon. Ottawa: Carleton UP, 1989. xvii–lviii.

– 'Mullins, Rosanna Eleanora (Leprohon).' *Dictionary of Canadian Biography*. Vol. 10 (1871 to 1880). Ed. Marc La Terreur. Toronto: U of Toronto P, 1972. 536–8.

Stouck, David. 'The Mirror and the Lamp in Sinclair Ross's *As for Me and My House*' (1974). In *Sinclair Ross's 'As for Me and My House': Five Decades of Criticism*. Ed. David Stouck. Toronto: U of Toronto P, 1991. 95–103.

– ed. *Sinclair Ross's 'As for Me and My House': Five Decades of Criticism*. Toronto: U of Toronto P, 1991.

Strange, Carolyn. *Toronto's Girl Problem: The Perils and Pleasures of the City, 1880–1930*. Toronto: U of Toronto P, 1995.

Strong-Boag, Veronica. 'Canadian Feminism in the 1920s: The Case of Nellie McClung.' *Journal of Canadian Studies* 12 (Summer 1977): 58–68.

– '"Ever a Crusader": Nellie McClung, First Wave Feminist.' In *Rethinking Canada: The Promise of Women's History*. Ed. Veronica Strong-Boag and Anita Clair Fellman. Toronto: Copp Clark Pitman, 1991. 308–21.

Tallman, Warren. 'Wolf in the Snow.' In *Contexts of Canadian Criticism*. Ed. Eli Mandel. Toronto: U of Toronto P, 1977. 232–53.

Thomas, Clara. Introduction. *The Canadian Settler's Guide*, by Catharine Parr Traill. Toronto: McClelland and Stewart, 1969.

– 'Journeys to Freedom.' *Canadian Literature* 51 (Winter 1972): 11–19.

Thompson, Elizabeth. *The Pioneer Woman: A Canadian Character Type*. Montreal: McGill-Queen's UP, 1991.

Thurston, John. 'Ideologies of the I: The Ideological Function of Life-Writing in Upper Canada.' *Wordsworth Circle* 25.1 (Winter 1994): 25–8.

– 'Re-writing *Roughing It*.' In *Future Indicative: Literary Theory and Canadian Literature*. Ed. John Moss. Ottawa: U of Ottawa P, 1987. 195–204.

– *The Work of Words: The Writing of Susanna Strickland Moodie*. Montreal: McGill-Queen's UP, 1996.

Tompkins, Jane. *Sensational Designs: The Cultural Work of American Fiction*. New York: Oxford UP, 1985.

– *West of Everything: The Inner Life of Westerns*. New York: Oxford UP, 1992.

Traill, Catharine Parr. *The Backwoods of Canada*. 1836. Toronto: McClelland and Stewart, 1989.

– *The Female Emigrant's Guide and Hints on Canadian Housekeeping.* Toronto: McClear and Co., 1854.

– 'Female Trials in the Bush.' *Sharpe's London Magazine* 15 (1852): 22–6.

Turner, Margaret E. *Imagining Culture: New World Narrative and the Writing of Canada.* Montreal: McGill-Queen's UP, 1995.

Valverde, Mariana. *The Age of Light, Soap and Water: Moral Reform in English Canada, 1885–1925.* Toronto: McClelland and Stewart, 1991.

Vipond, Mary. 'Bestsellers in English Canada, 1899–1918: An Overview.' *Journal of Canadian Fiction* 24 (1979): 96–119.

– 'Bestsellers in English Canada, 1919–1928.' *Journal of Canadian Fiction* 35–6 (1986): 73–105.

Warne, Randi R. *Literature as Pulpit: The Christian Social Activism of Nellie L. McClung.* Waterloo, Ont.: Canadian Corporation for Studies in Religion / Wilfrid Laurier UP, 1993.

Williams, David. 'The "Scarlet" Rompers: Toward a New Perspective in *As for Me and My House.*' *Canadian Literature* 103 (Winter 1984): 156–66.

Wood, Joanna E. *Judith Moore; or, Fashioning a Pipe.* Toronto: Ontario Publishing Company, 1898.

– *The Untempered Wind.* 1894. Intro. Klay Dyer. Ottawa: Tecumseh, 1994.

Index

gender, 4, 18, 21–2; defined, 6–9;
hierarchy, 14, 61, 72–3, 107, 109,
110; identification, 8; as ideology, 9,
107–8; and narrative of liberation,
5, 9, 13, 16, 18, 58–9; as performative, 6–8; and subjectivity, 7–8, 18,
107–8; as textual practice, 7–9, 11,
18, 107–8. *See also* femininity
Genette, Gérard, 11
Gerson, Carole, 58, 59, 60, 118n8
Gilbert, Sandra, 105–6
Glickman, Susan, 36
Godard, Barbara, 59
Golden Dog, The (Kirby), 43–4
gossip, 36, 39–40, 41
Gubar, Susan, 105–6

heterosexuality. *See* marriage; sexual
contract
historical context, importance of, 4–5,
6, 9, 105
historical romance. *See* romance, historical
home, 3–4, 21, 24, 25–6, 32, 33, 73–4,
79–80, 97–9

idealism, 68–9, 70–1, 92–3
ideology: defined, 8–9; femininity as,
4, 6, 9, 12–13, 18–28, 33–4, 60–1,
62–3, 92, 108, 109–10; gender as, 9;
liberal, 79; realism as, 4, 10–11
illness, 51–2, 63
immigration. *See* emigration
imperialism, translated as gender relations, 42–3, 55–6
inner self. *See* self, inner
intelligence, and feminine ideal,
37–8, 116n11, 116–17n12
interpellation, 4, 8, 108
interrogative text, 94, 95

intuition, 95–6
Irigaray, Luce, 110

Jackel, Susan, 28
Judith Moore; or, Fashioning a Pipe
(Wood), 63–6

Kerchiefs to Hunt Souls (Fytche), 59,
70–2, 108
Kirby, William: *The Golden Dog*, 43–4
Kroetsch, Robert, 105, 106, 123n14

labour, women's, 16, 17, 22–6, 27–8,
73–4, 75, 79–80, 87
Ladha, Yasmin, 61
language: as law, 80–1; and subjectivity, 7–9, 81, 82, 110; women's
ambivalent relation to, 81–4
Leprohon, Rosanna, 5, 11, 107, 108,
112–13n5; *Antoinette de Mirecourt*,
13–14, 42–6, 48–56, 108, 109;
Armand Durand, 47–8
Letters of a Lifetime (Moodie), 31
liberal ideology, 79
liberation, narrative of, 5, 9, 13, 16,
18, 58–9
Life in the Clearings (Moodie), 30, 31,
37–40

McClung, Nellie, 5, 11, 14, 77–80,
83–93, 107, 108–9; 'Carried Forward,' 80, 90; *Clearing in the West*,
84–5, 87, 88–91, 92; 'Neutral Fuse,'
84, 86, 87; *Painted Fires*, 82–3, 84,
91, 121n5; *Purple Springs*, 80–2, 84,
90; *Sowing Seeds in Danny*, 84; *The
Stream Runs Fast*, 87, 89, 90, 91, 92;
'The Writer's Creed,' 77
McDonald, Larry, 6
MacMillan, Carrie, 5, 58–9, 119n7